FOR ORGANS, PIANOS & ELECTRONIC KEYBOARDS

E-Z PLAY TODAY

129

Campfire Songs

ISBN 978-1-4950-0794-1

DISTRIBUTED BY

HAL•LEONARD®
CORPORATION

7777 W. BLUEMOUND RD. P.O.BOX 13819 MILWAUKEE, WI 53213

E-Z Play® Today Music Notation © 1975 by HAL LEONARD CORPORATION
E-Z PLAY and EASY ELECTRONIC KEYBOARD MUSIC are registered trademarks of HAL LEONARD CORPORATION.

Visit Hal Leonard Online at
www.halleonard.com

Amie

Registration 4
Rhythm: Country or Swing

Words and Music by
Craig Fuller

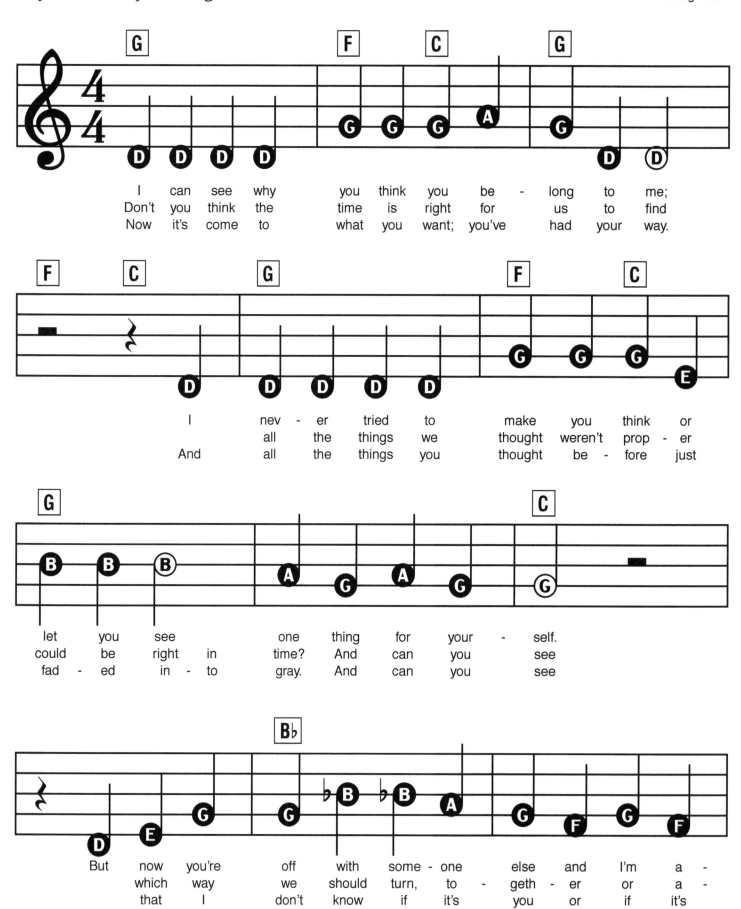

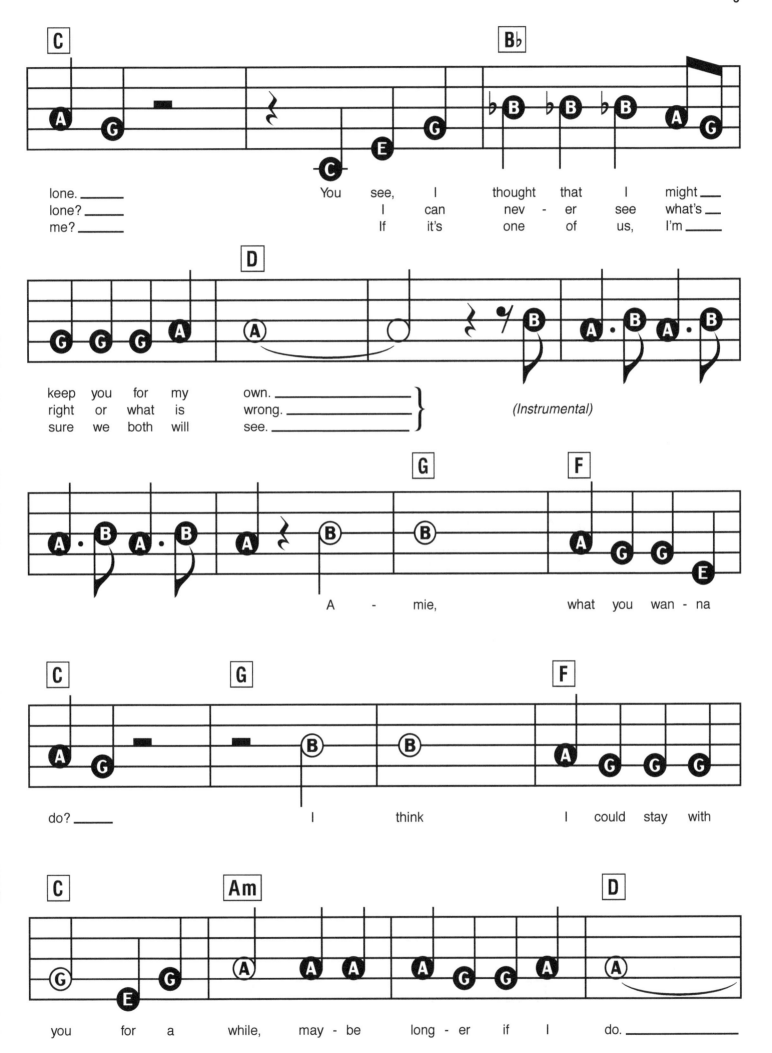

6

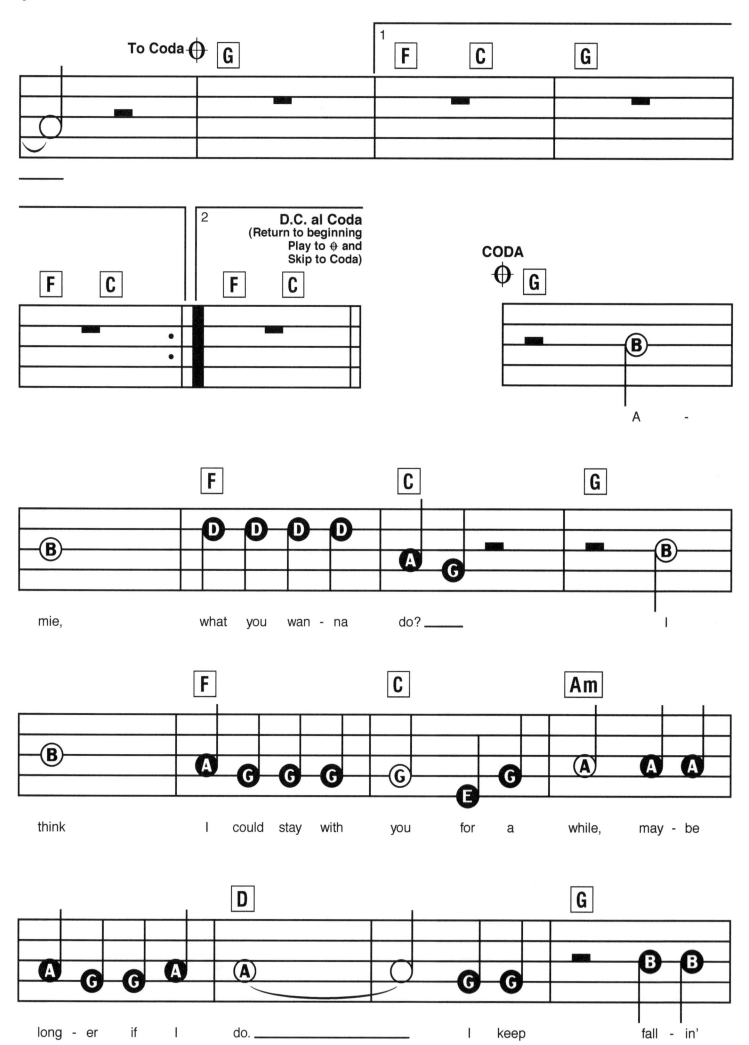

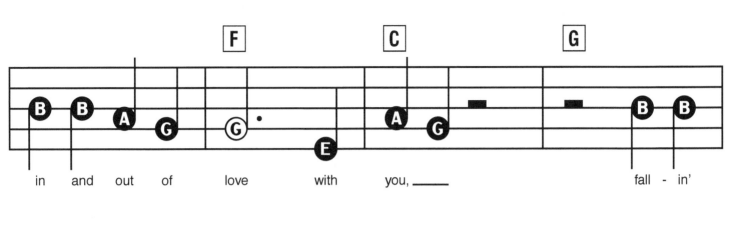

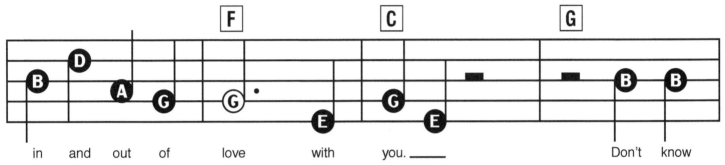

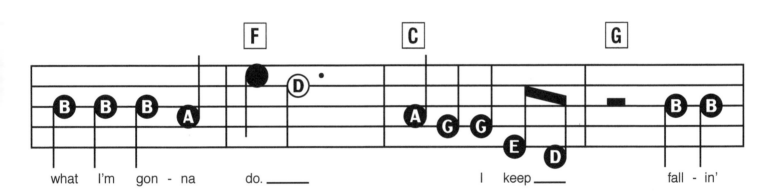

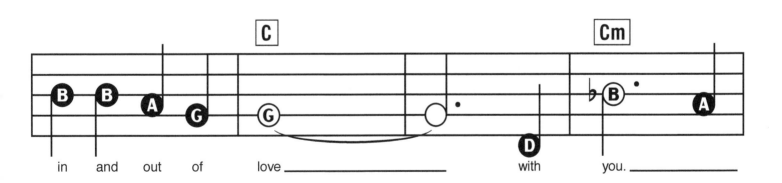

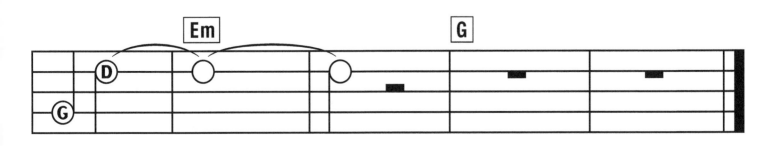

Blowin' in the Wind

Registration 4
Rhythm: Ballad or Fox Trot

Words and Music by
Bob Dylan

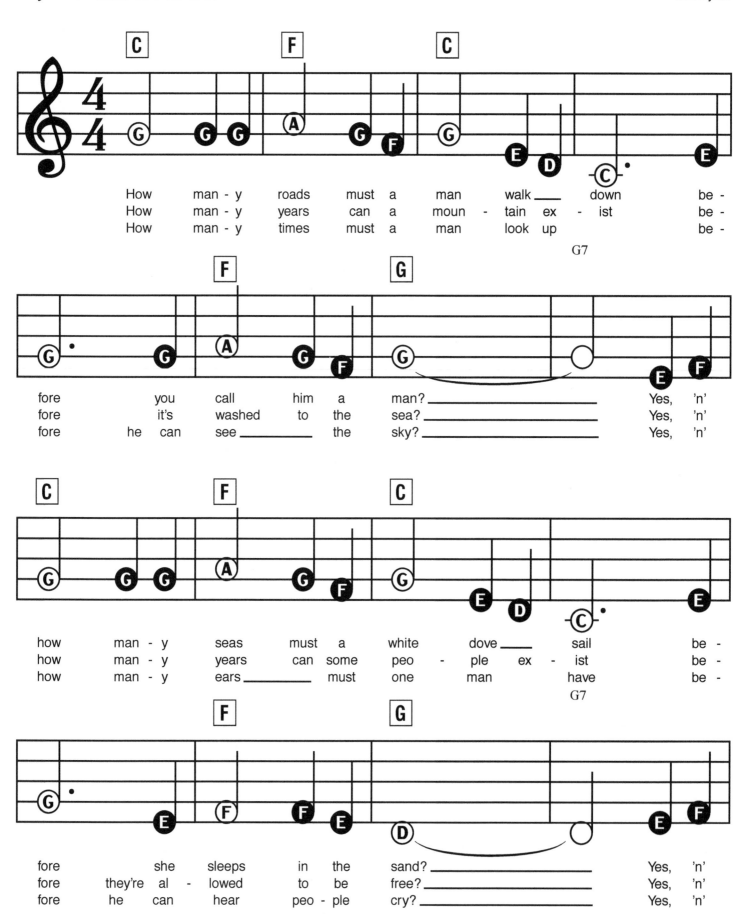

Brown Eyed Girl

Registration 1
Rhythm: 8-Beat or Rock

Words and Music by
Van Morrison

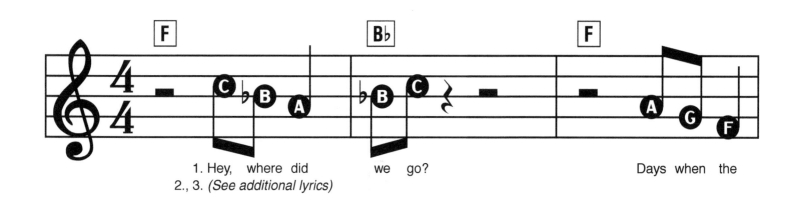

1. Hey, where did we go? Days when the
2., 3. (See additional lyrics)

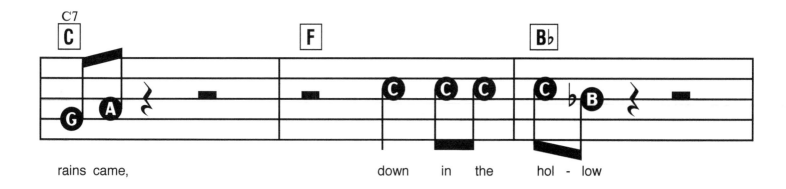

rains came, down in the hol - low

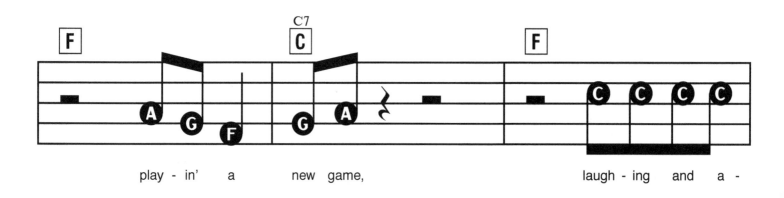

play - in' a new game, laugh - ing and a -

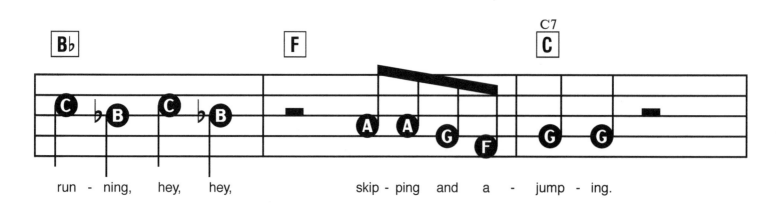

run - ning, hey, hey, skip - ping and a - jump - ing.

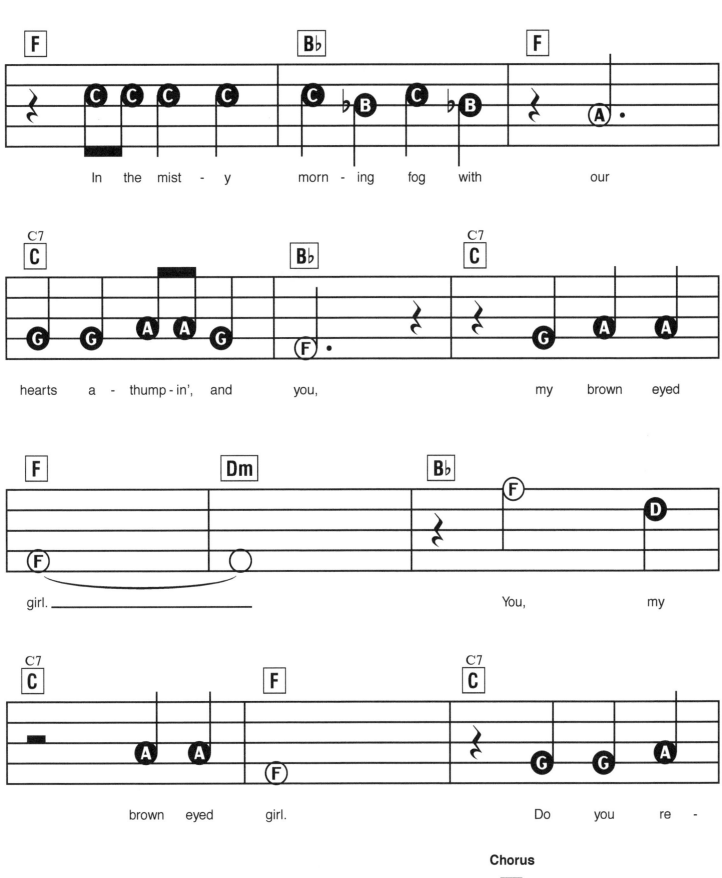

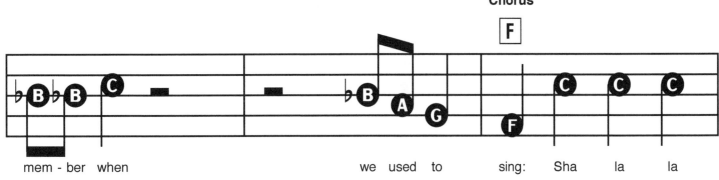

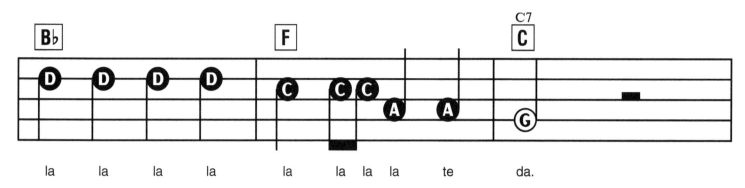

la   la   la   la   la   la la la   te   da.

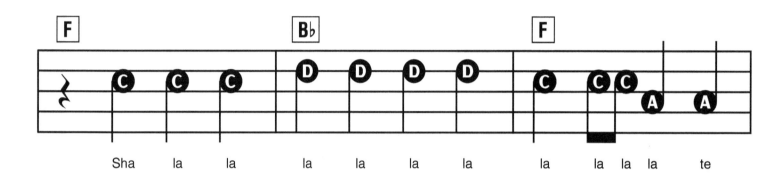

Sha   la   la   la   la   la   la   la   la la la   te

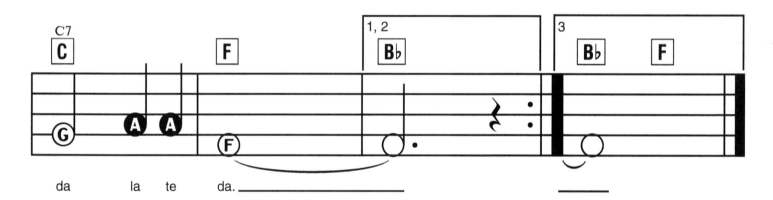

da   la   te   da. _____

Additional Lyrics

2. Whatever happened to Tuesday and so slow
   Going down the old mine with a transistor radio,
   Standing in the sunlight laughing,
   Hiding behind a rainbow's wall,
   Slipping and a-sliding
   All along the waterfall
   With you, my brown eyed girl.
   You, my brown eyed girl.
   Do you remember when we used to sing:
   Chorus

3. So hard to find my way, now that I'm all on my own.
   I saw you just the other day. My, how you have grown.
   Cast my memory back there, Lord.
   Sometime I'm overcome thinking 'bout
   Making love in the green grass
   Behind the stadium
   With you, my brown eyed girl,
   With you, my brown eyed girl.
   Do you remember when we used to sing:
   Chorus

The Campfire Song Song
from SPONGEBOB SQUAREPANTS

Registration 4
Rhythm: Fast Rock

Words and Music by Carl Williams,
Dan Povenmire, Jay Lender,
Michael Culross and Michael Walker

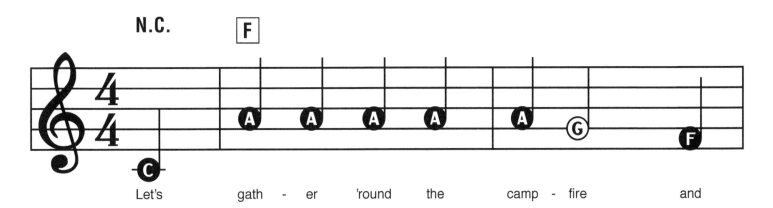

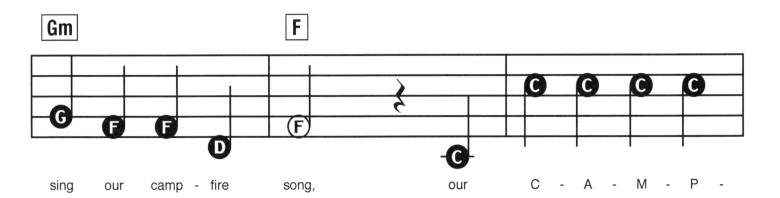

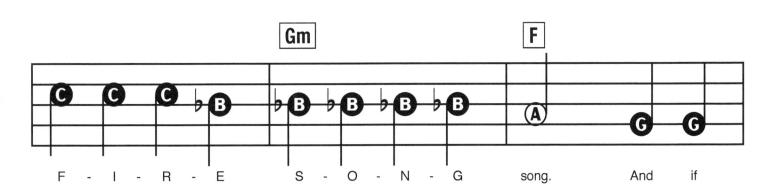

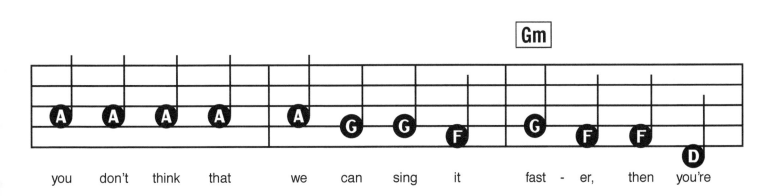

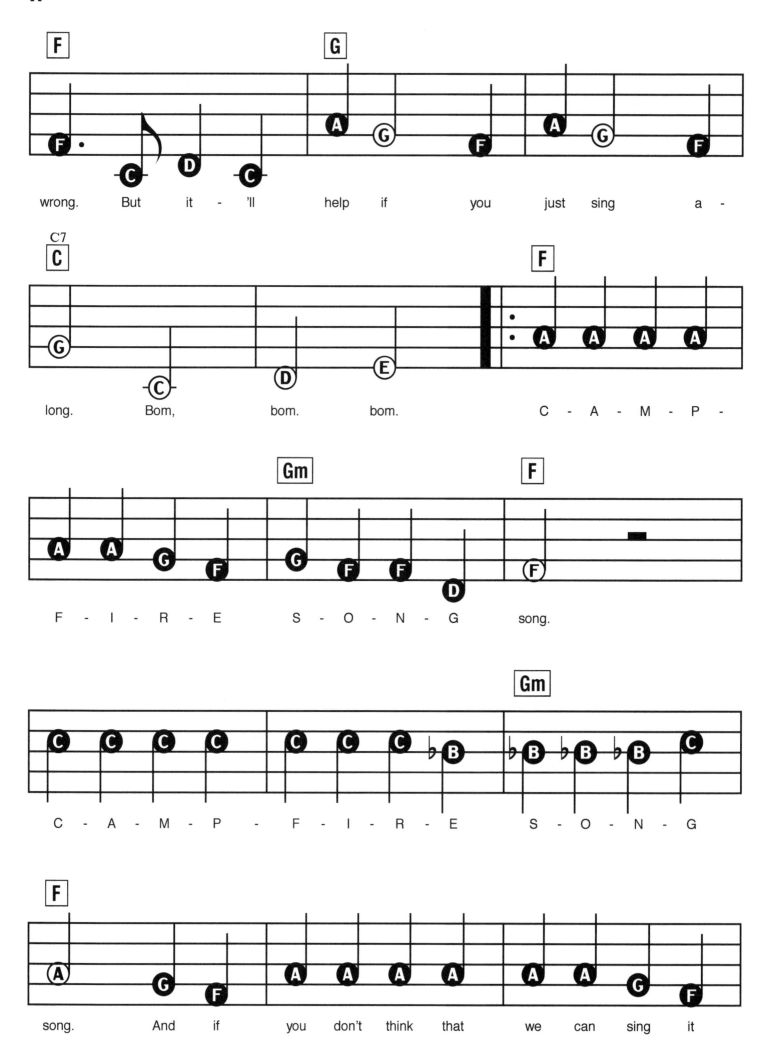

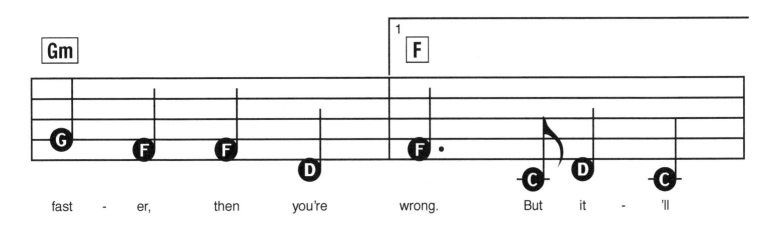

fast - er, then you're wrong. But it - 'll

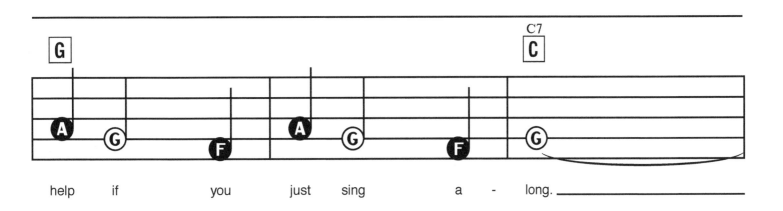

help if you just sing a - long.

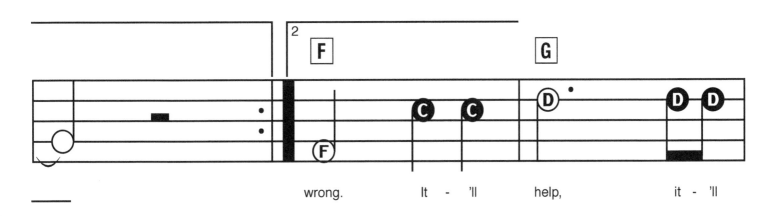

wrong. It - 'll help, it - 'll

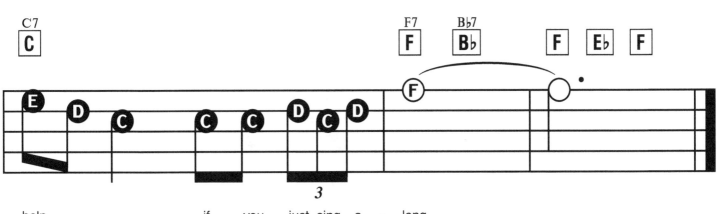

help _____ if you just sing a - long. _____

Don't Worry, Be Happy

Registration 5
Rhythm: Calypso

Words and Music by
Bobby McFerrin

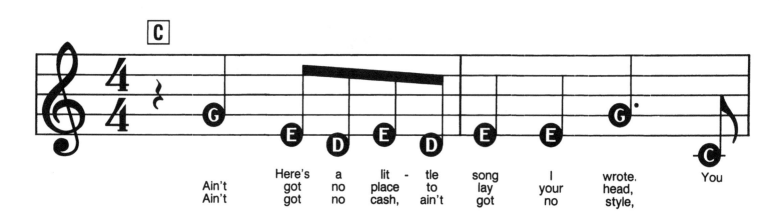

Ain't
Here's a lit - tle song I wrote. You
got no place to lay your head,
got no cash, ain't got no style,

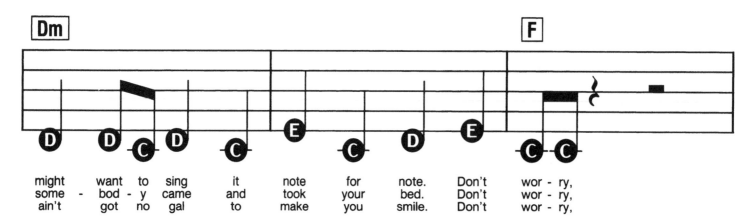

might want to sing it note for note. Don't wor - ry,
some - bod - y came and took your bed. Don't wor - ry,
ain't got no gal to make you smile. Don't wor - ry,

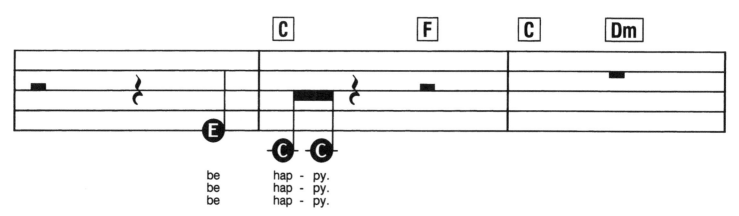

be hap - py.
be hap - py.
be hap - py.

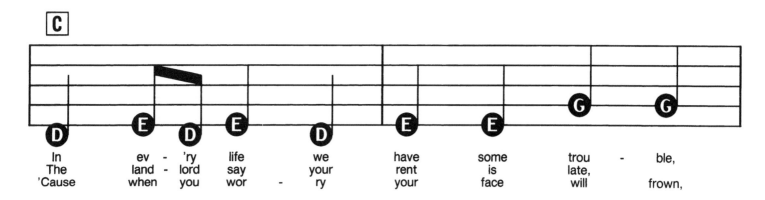

In ev - 'ry life we have some trou - ble,
The land - lord say your rent is late,
'Cause when you wor - ry your face will frown,

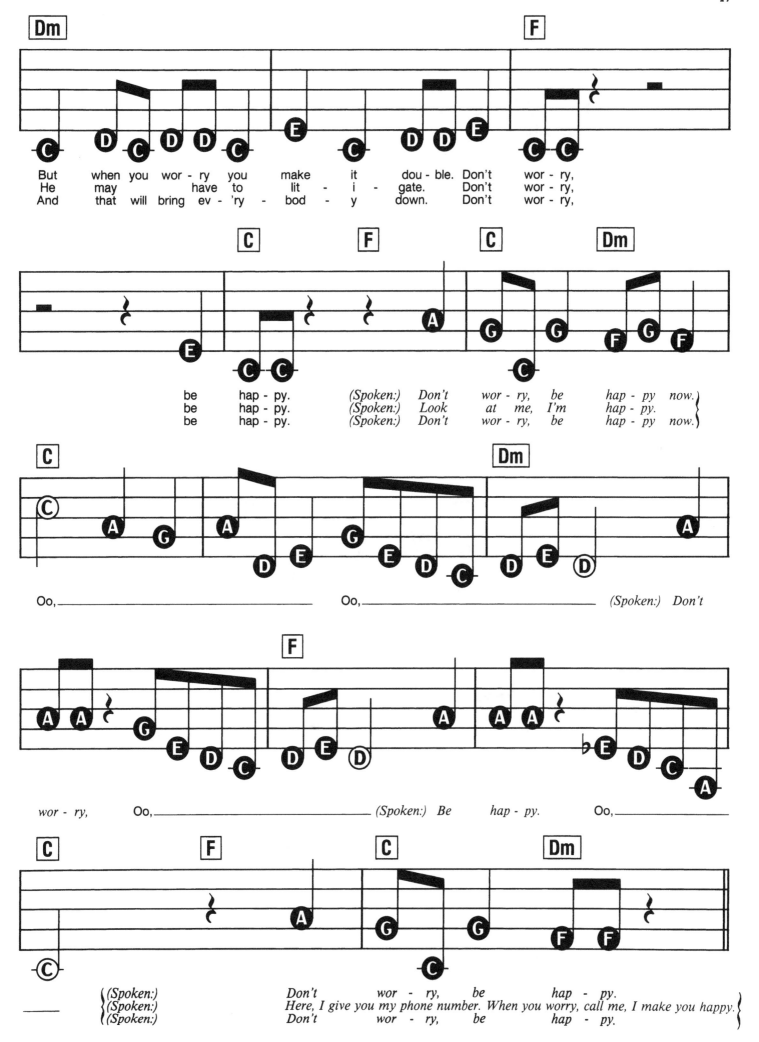

18

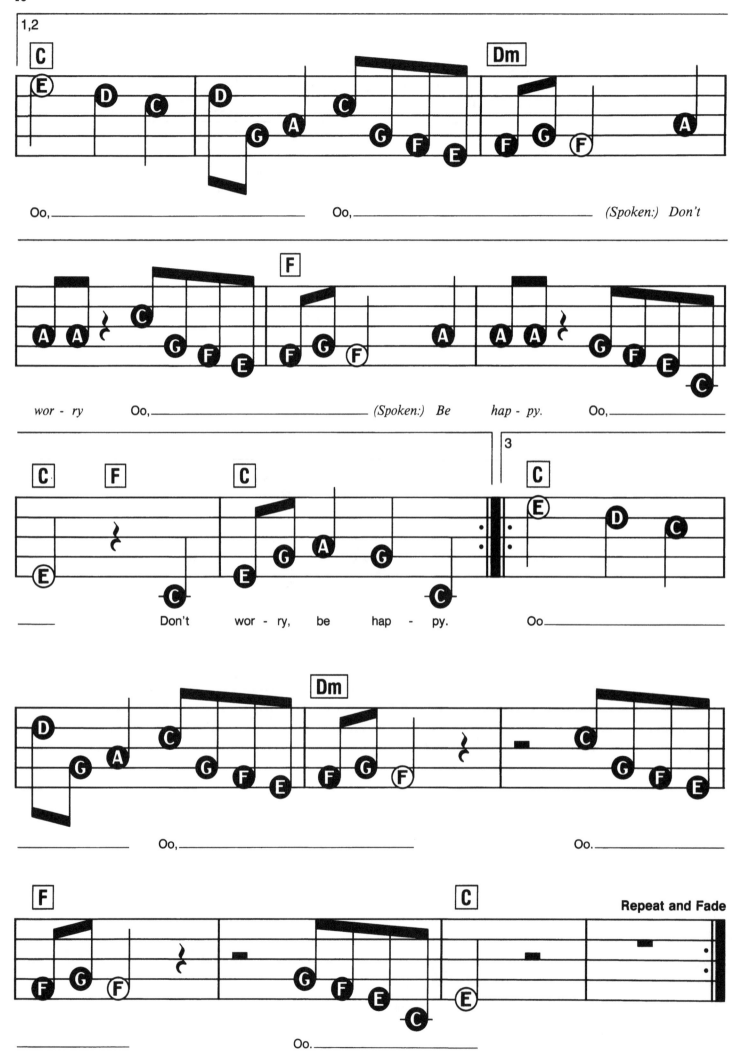

Drift Away

Registration 8
Rhythm: Pop or 8-Beat

Words and Music by
Mentor Williams

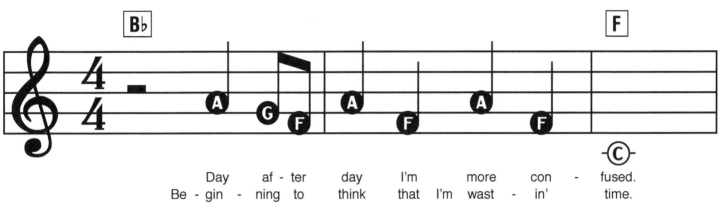

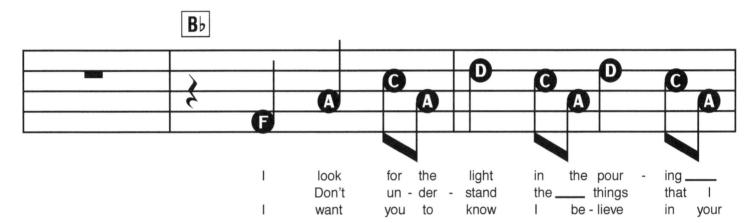

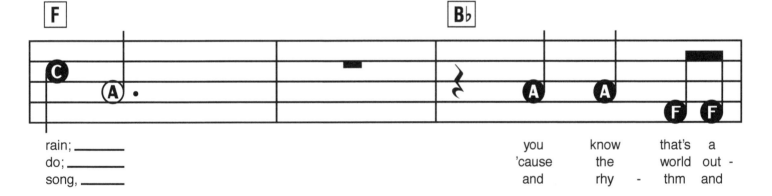

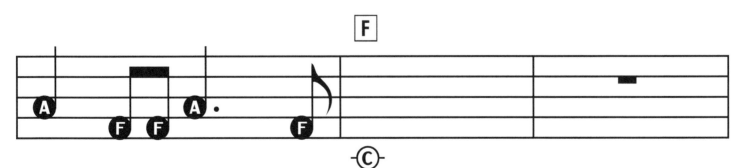

20

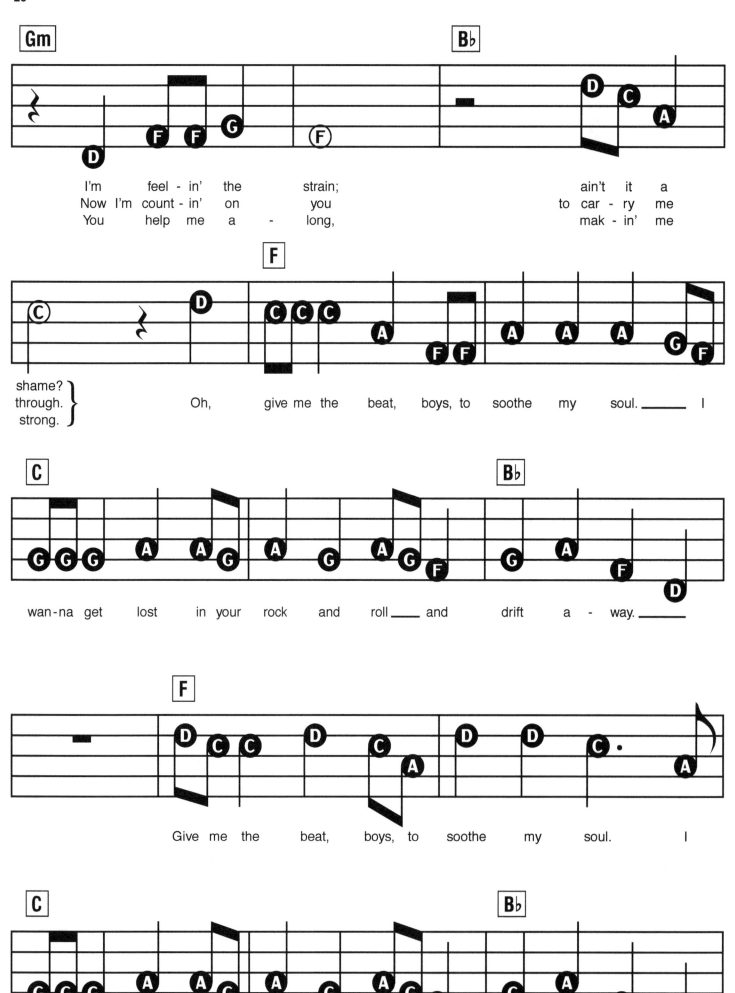

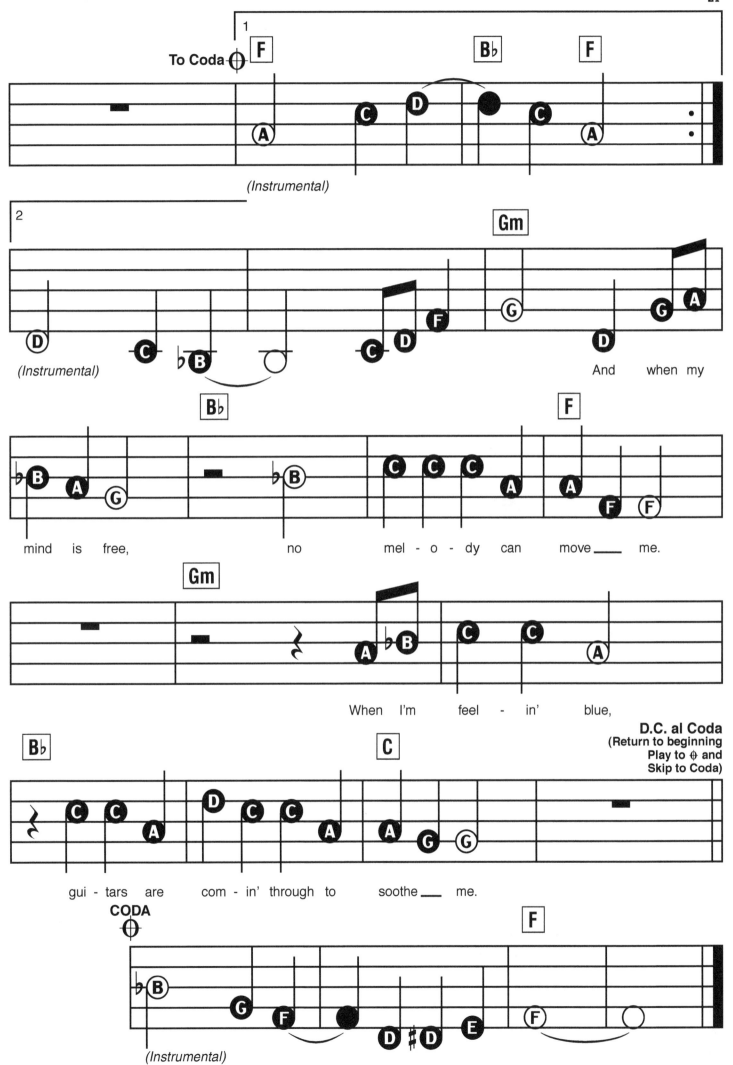

Edelweiss
from THE SOUND OF MUSIC

Registration 4
Rhythm: Waltz

Lyrics by Oscar Hammerstein II
Music by Richard Rodgers

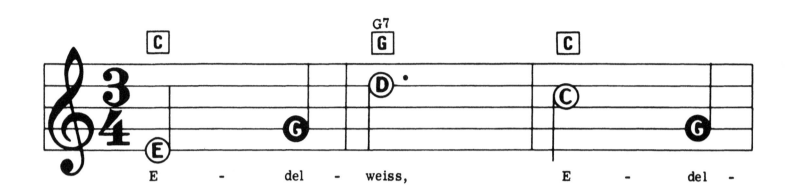

E - del - weiss, E - del -

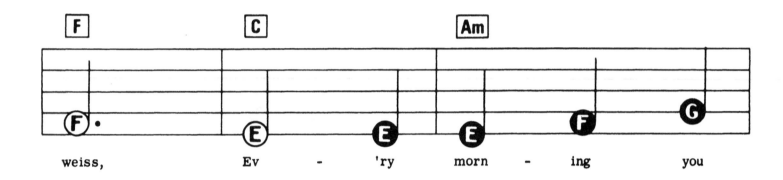

weiss, Ev - 'ry morn - ing you

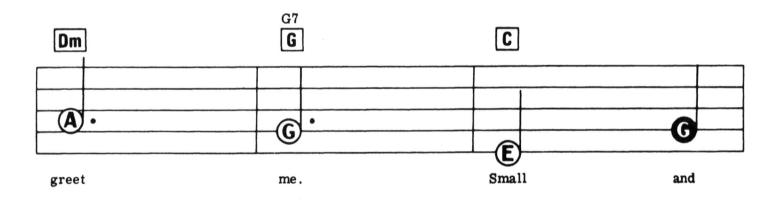

greet me. Small and

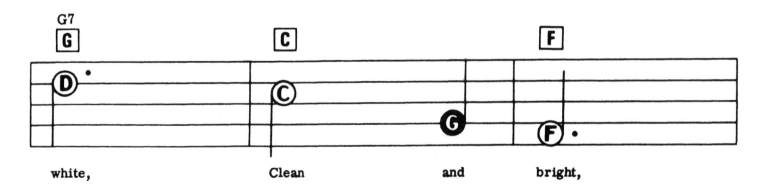

white, Clean and bright,

23

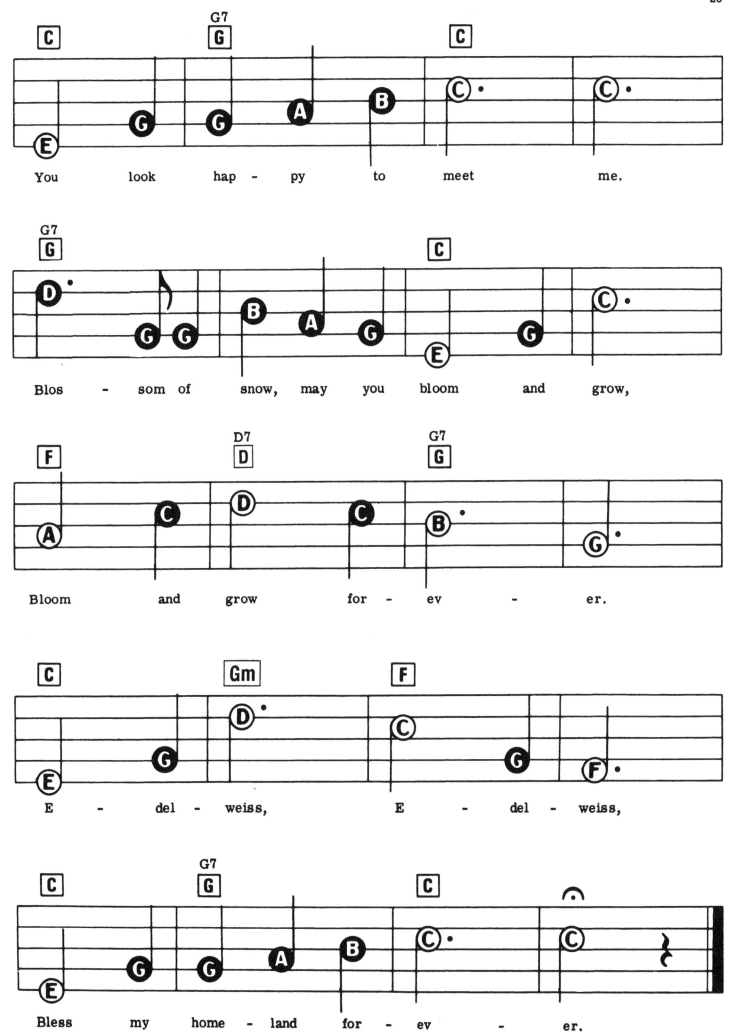

Folsom Prison Blues

Registration 3
Rhythm: Rock or Fox Trot

Words and Music by
John R. Cash

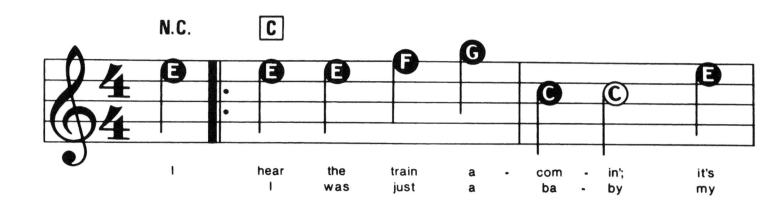

I hear the train a - com - in'; it's
I was just a ba - by my

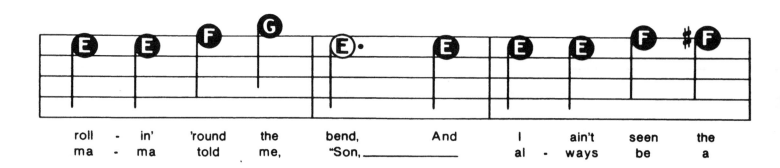

roll - in' 'round the bend, And I ain't seen the
ma - ma told me, "Son,_____ al - ways be a

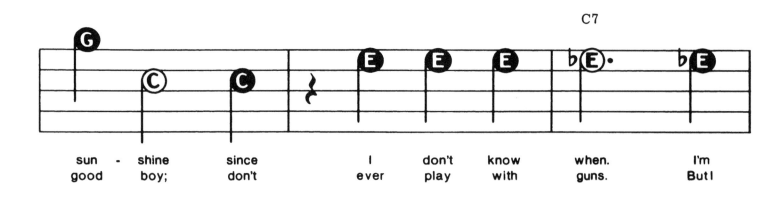

C7

sun - shine since I don't know when. I'm
good boy; since don't ever play with guns. But I

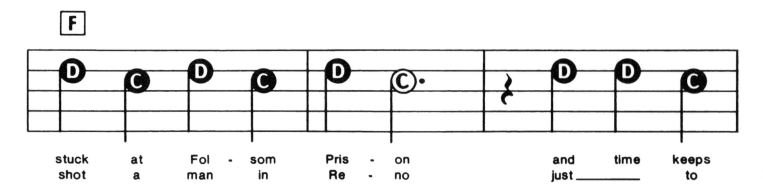

F

stuck at Fol - som Pris - on and time keeps
shot a man in Re - no just_____ to

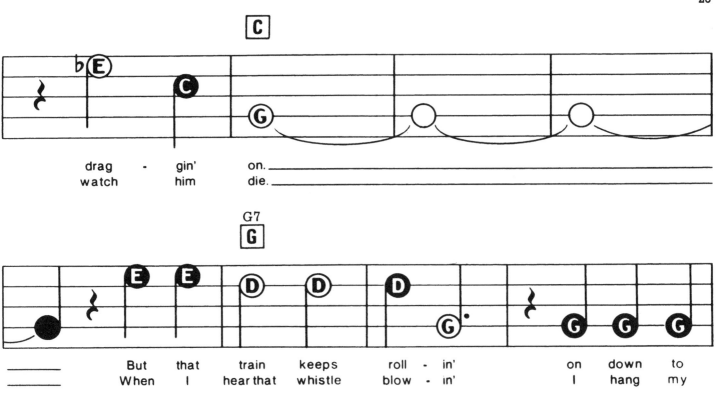

drag - gin' on. _____
watch him die. _____

_____ But that train keeps roll - in' on down to
_____ When I hear that whistle blow - in' I hang my

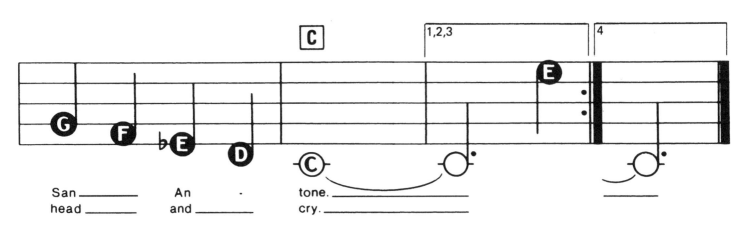

San _____ An - tone. _____
head _____ and _____ cry. _____

3. I bet there's rich folks eatin' in a fancy dining car.
They're prob'ly drinkin' coffee and smokin' big cigars,
But I know I had it comin', I know I can't be free,
But those people keep a-movin', and that's what tortures me.

4. Well, if they freed me from this prison, if that railroad train was mine,
I bet I'd move over a little farther down the line,
Far from Folsom Prison, that's where I want to stay.
And I'd let that lonesome whistle blow my blues away.

The Gambler

Registration 7
Rhythm: Country or Swing

Words and Music by
Don Schlitz

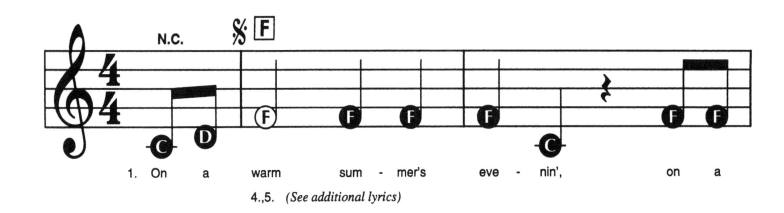

1. On a warm sum-mer's eve-nin', on a
4.,5. *(See additional lyrics)*

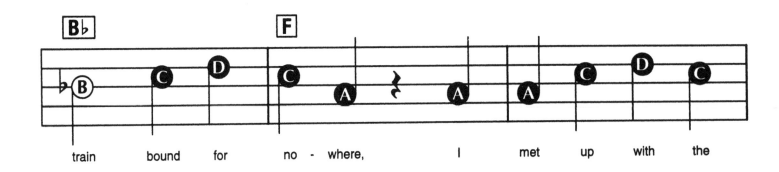

train bound for no - where, I met up with the

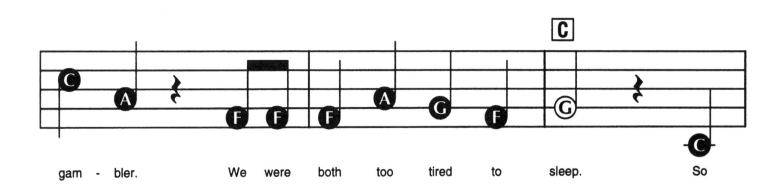

gam - bler. We were both too tired to sleep. So

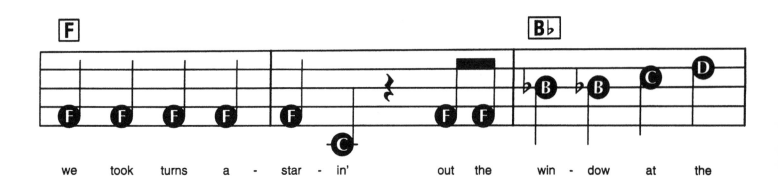

we took turns a - star - in' out the win - dow at the

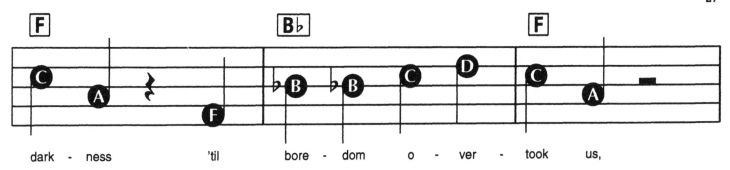

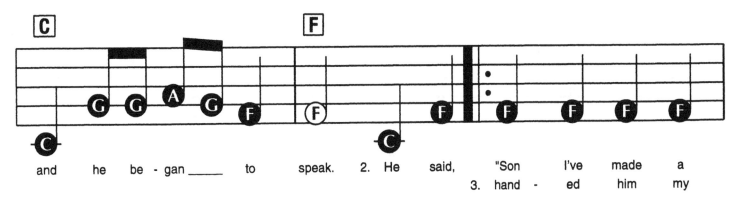

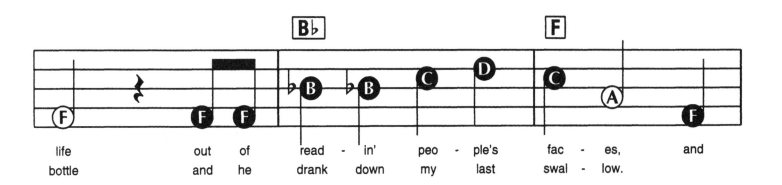

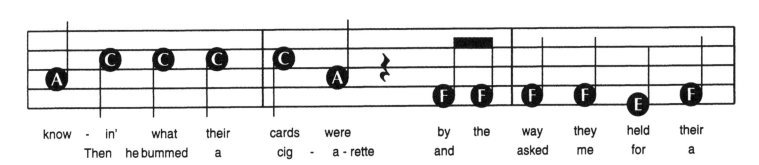

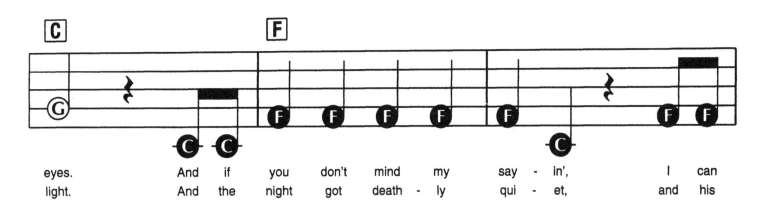

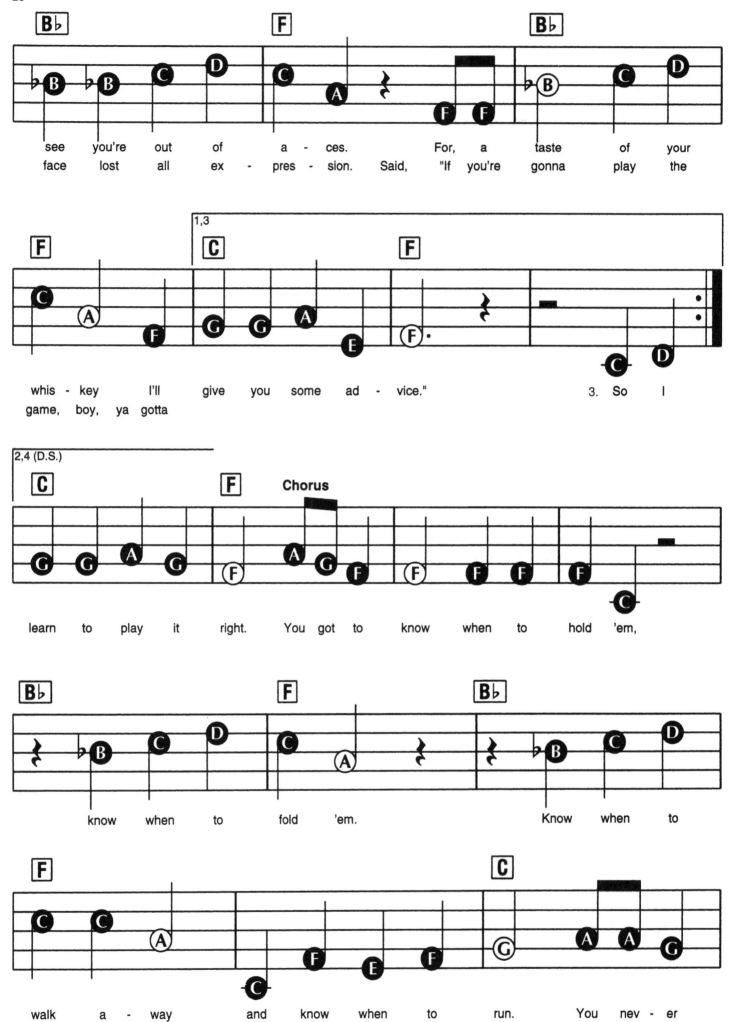

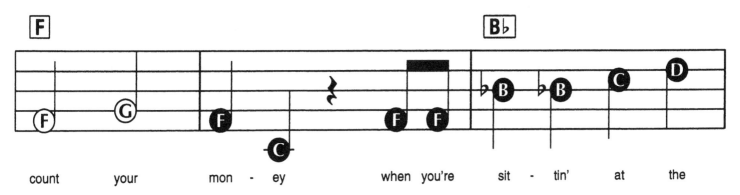

count your mon - ey when you're sit - tin' at the

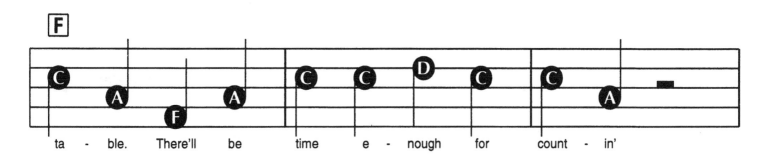

ta - ble. There'll be time e - nough for count - in'

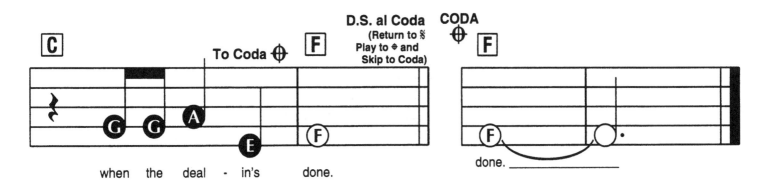

when the deal - in's done.

done. _____

Additional Lyrics

4. "Every gambler knows that the secret to survivin'
Is knowin' what to throw away
And knowin' what to keep.
'Cause every hand's a winner and every hand's a loser.
And the best that you can hope for is to die in your sleep."

5. And when he'd finished speakin', he turned back towards the window,
Crushed out his cigarette and faded off to sleep.
And somewhere in the darkness the gambler, he broke even.
But in his final words I found an ace that I could keep.

To Chorus

God Bless the U.S.A.

Registration 4
Rhythm: Country or 8-Beat

Words and Music by
Lee Greenwood

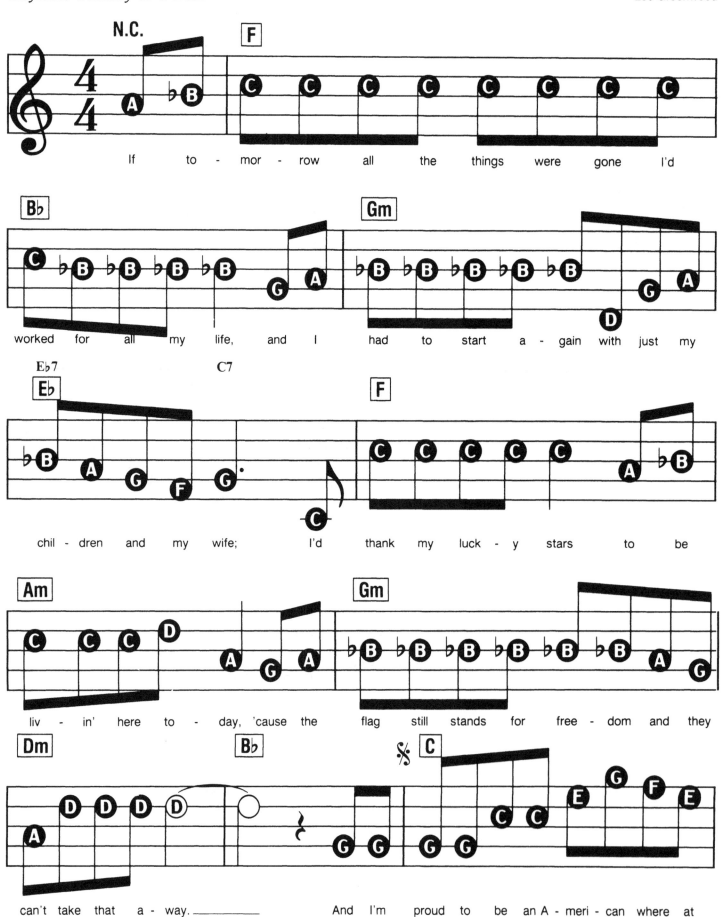

31

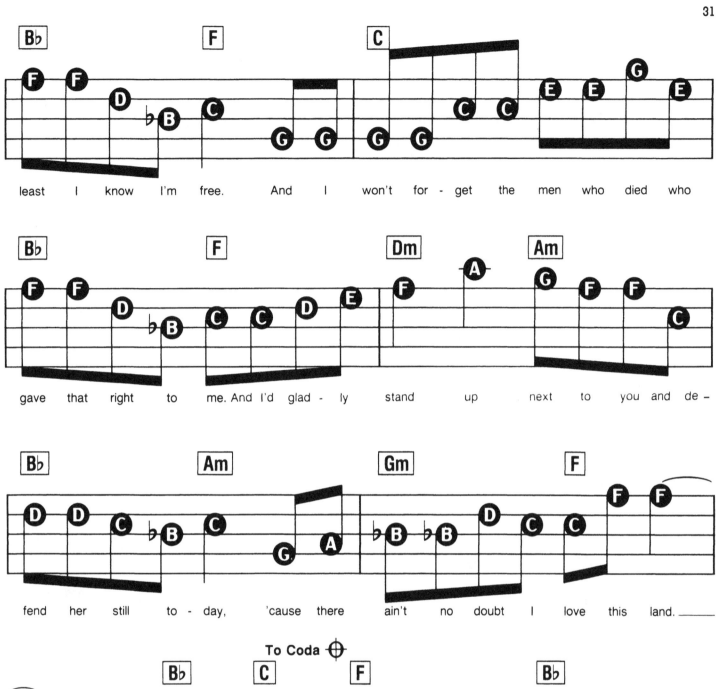

least I know I'm free. And I won't for - get the men who died who

gave that right to me. And I'd glad - ly stand up next to you and de -

fend her still to - day, 'cause there ain't no doubt I love this land. _____

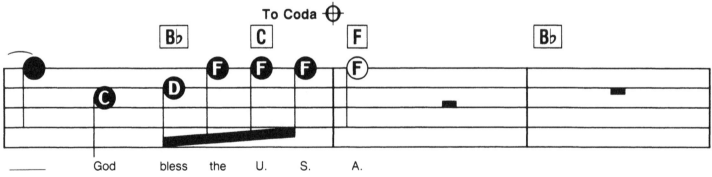

To Coda

_____ God bless the U. S. A.

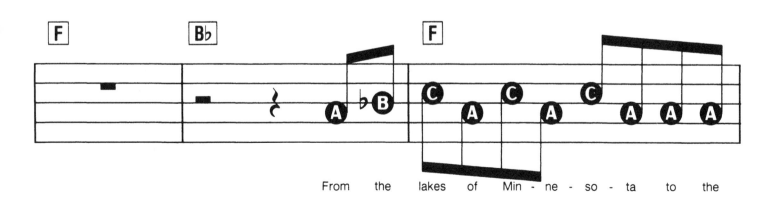

From the lakes of Min - ne - so - ta to the

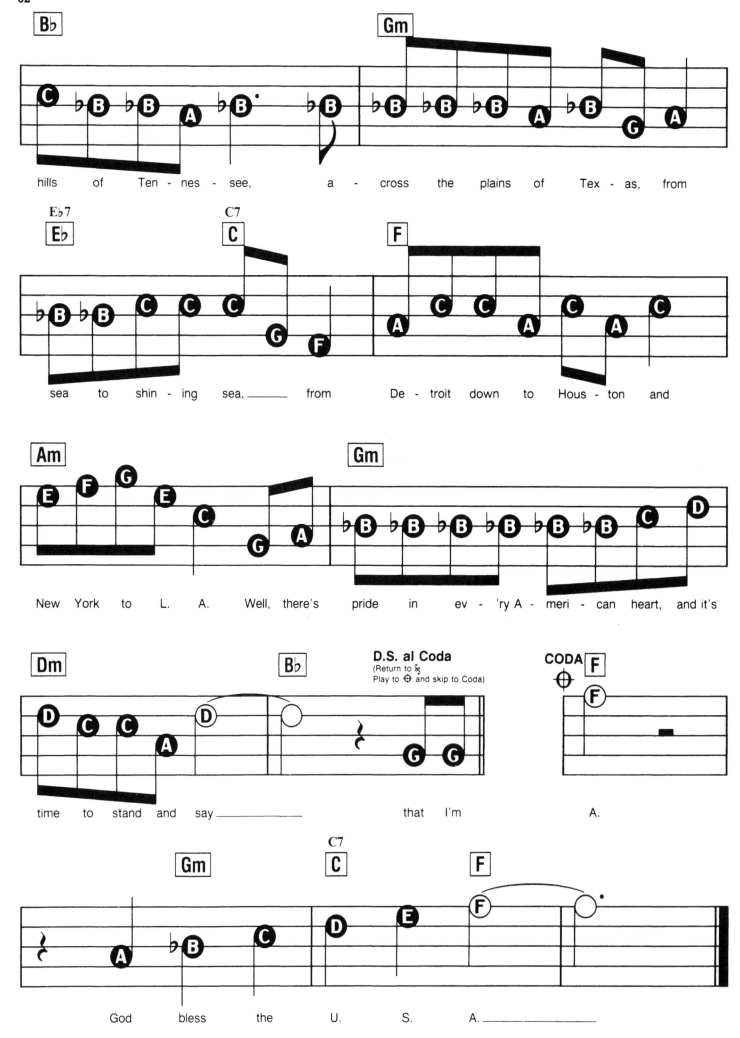

Heart and Soul

Registration 8
Rhythm: Swing

Words by Frank Loesser
Music by Hoagy Carmichael

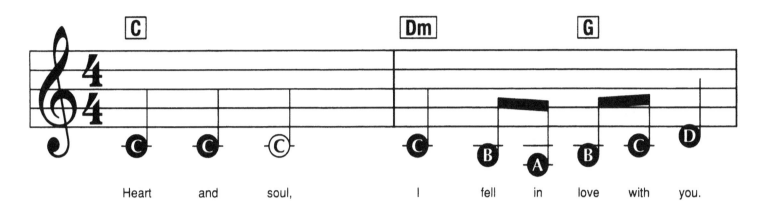

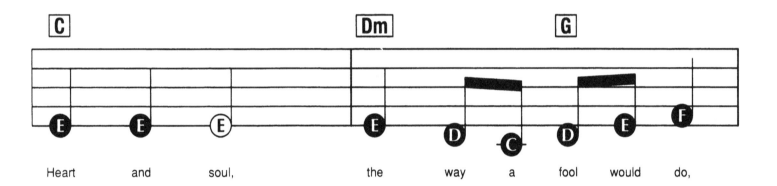

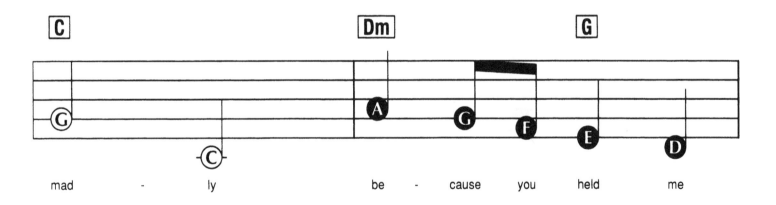

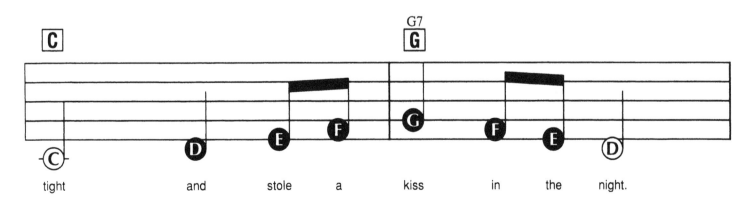

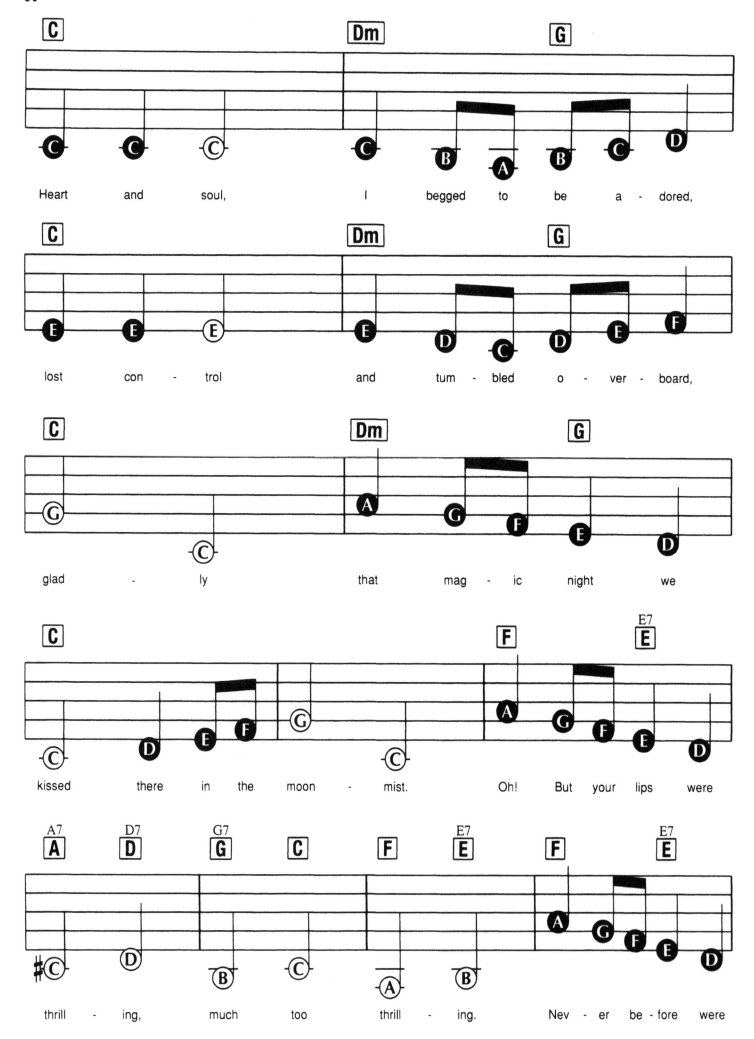

Hallelujah

Registration 4
Rhythm: 6/8 March

Words and Music by
Leonard Cohen

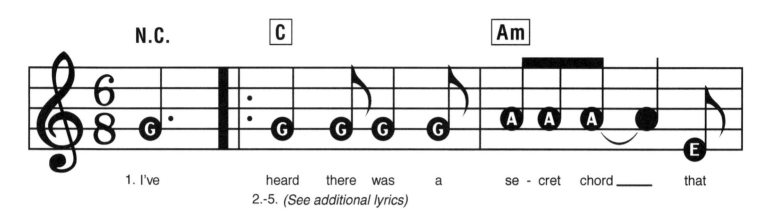

1. I've heard there was a se - cret chord ____ that
2.-5. *(See additional lyrics)*

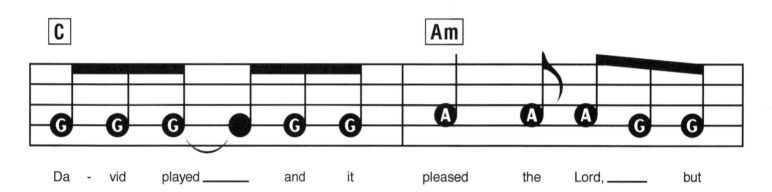

Da - vid played ____ and it pleased the Lord, ____ but

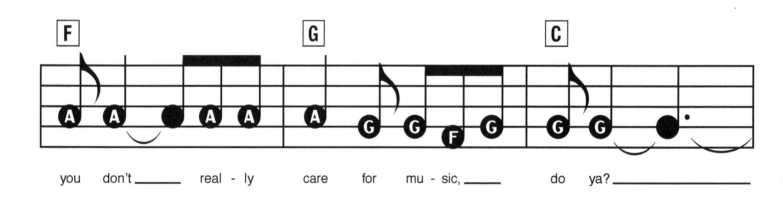

you don't ____ real - ly care for mu - sic, ____ do ya? ____

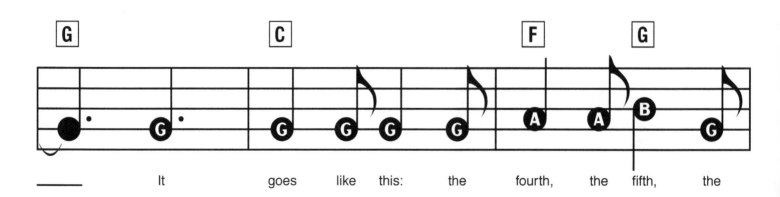

____ It goes like this: the fourth, the fifth, the

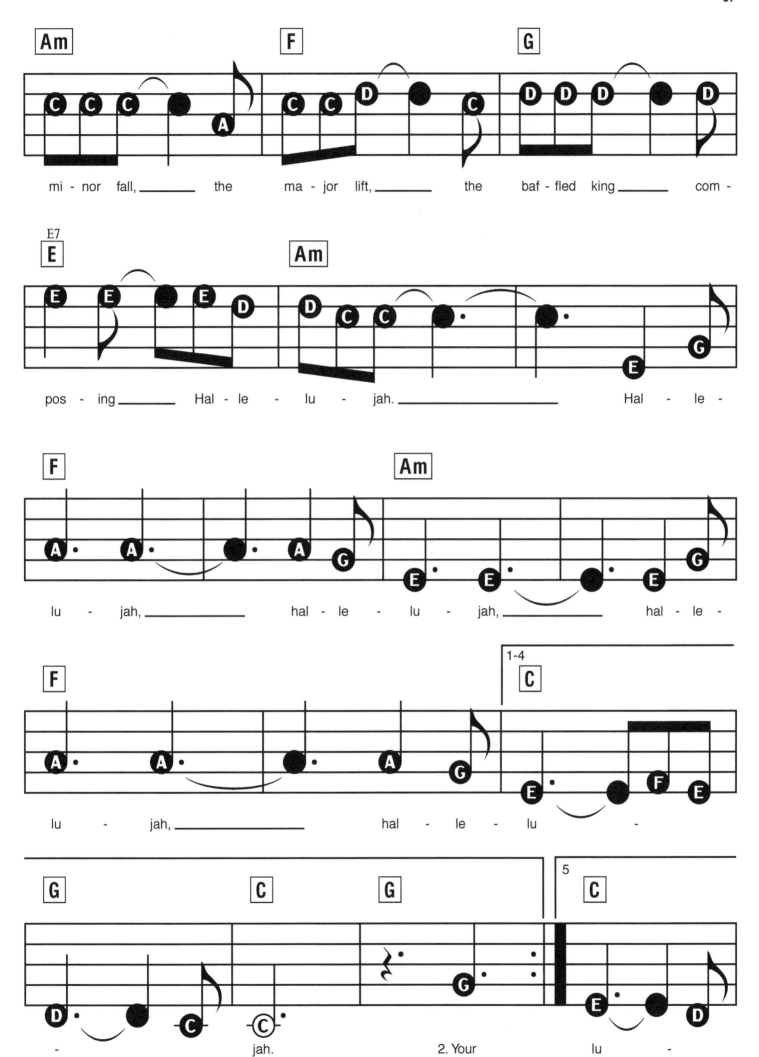

38

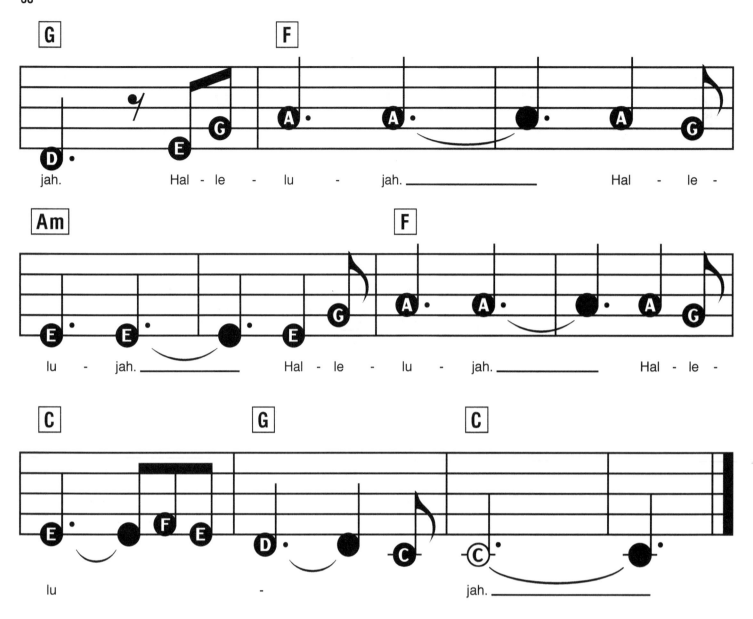

Additional Lyrics

2. Your faith was strong but you needed proof.
   You saw her bathing on the roof.
   Her beauty and the moonlight overthrew ya.
   She tied you to a kitchen chair.
   She broke your throne, she cut your hair.
   And from your lips she drew the Hallelujah.

3. Maybe I have been here before.
   I know this room, I've walked this floor.
   I used to live alone before I knew ya.
   I've seen your flag on the marble arch.
   Love is not a vict'ry march.
   It's a cold and it's a broken Hallelujah.

4. There was a time you let me know
   What's real and going on below.
   But now you never show it to me, do ya?
   And remember when I moved in you.
   The holy dark was movin', too,
   And every breath we drew was Hallelujah.

5. Maybe there's a God above,
   And all I ever learned from love
   Was how to shoot at someone who outdrew ya.
   And it's not a cry you can hear at night.
   It's not somebody who's seen the light.
   It's a cold and it's a broken Hallelujah.

Lean on Me

Registration 8
Rhythm: Rock or 8-Beat

Words and Music by
Bill Withers

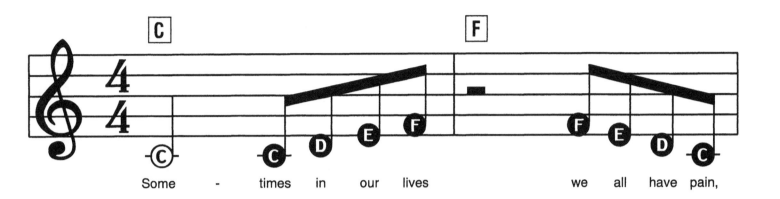

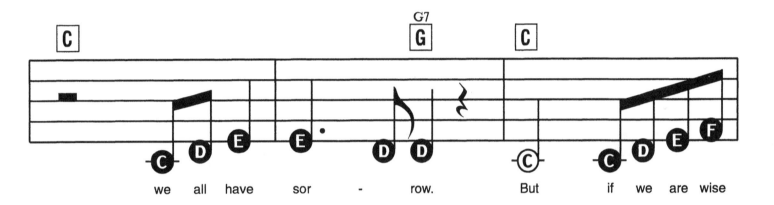

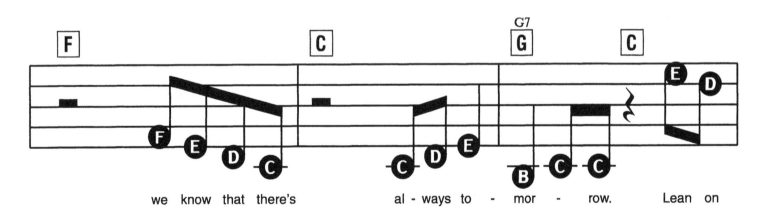

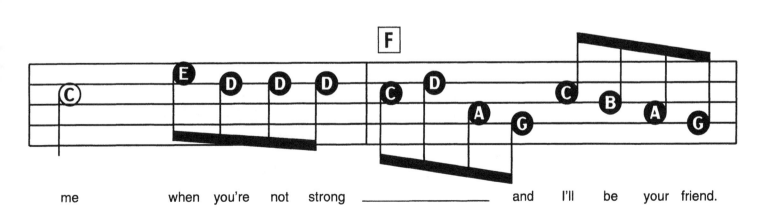

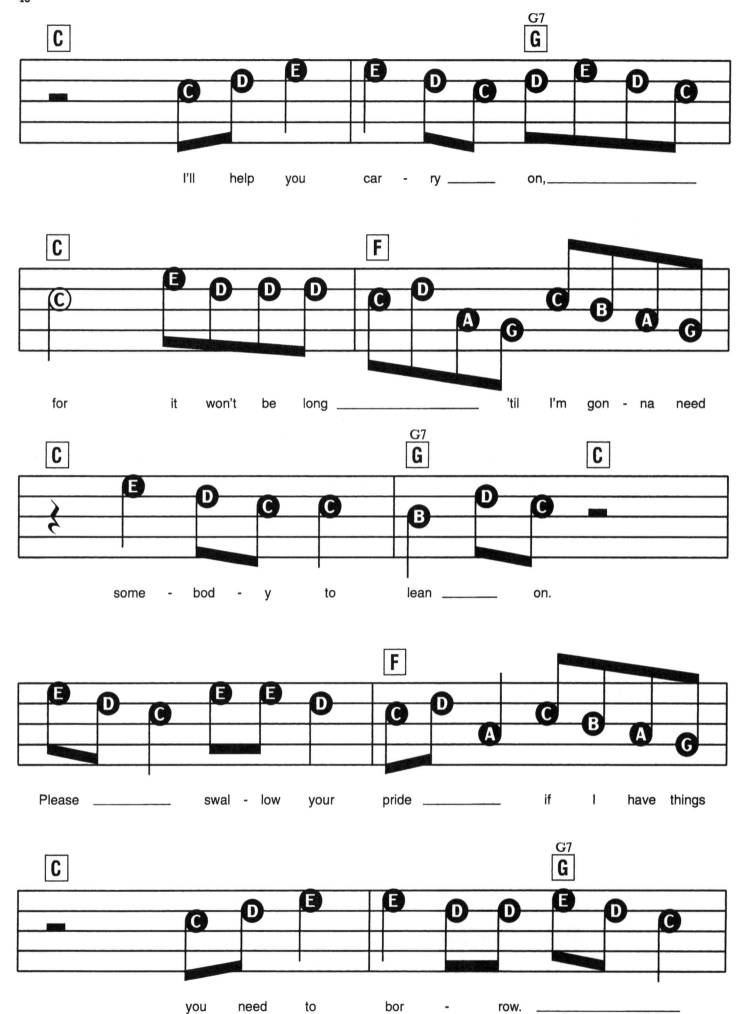

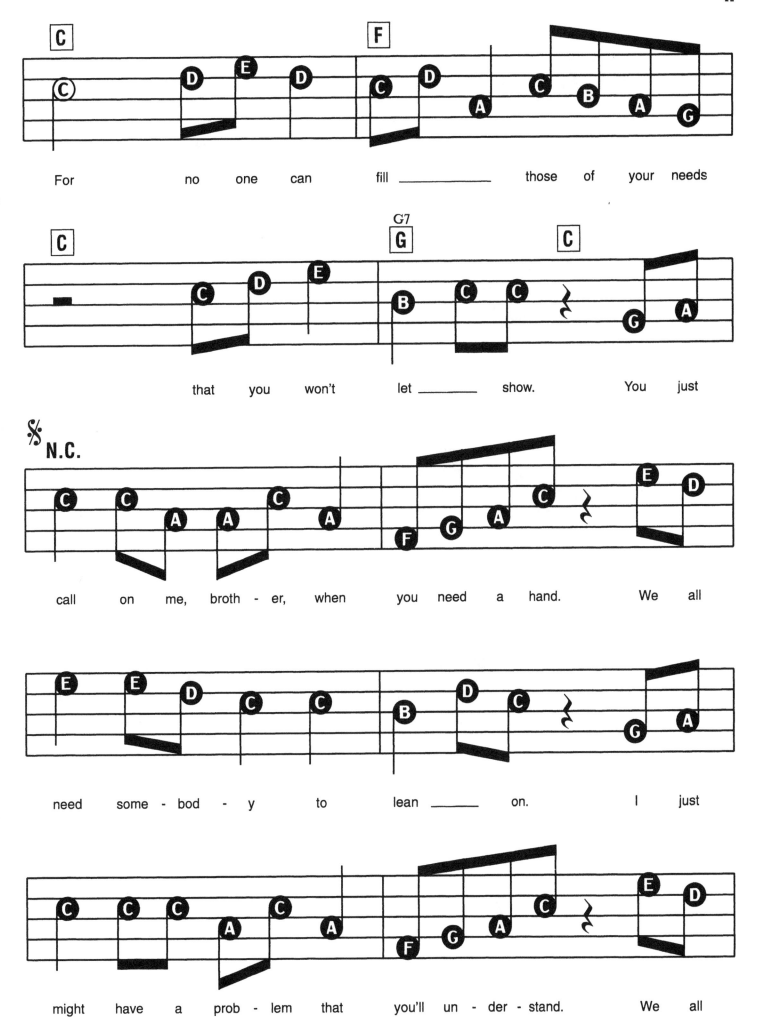

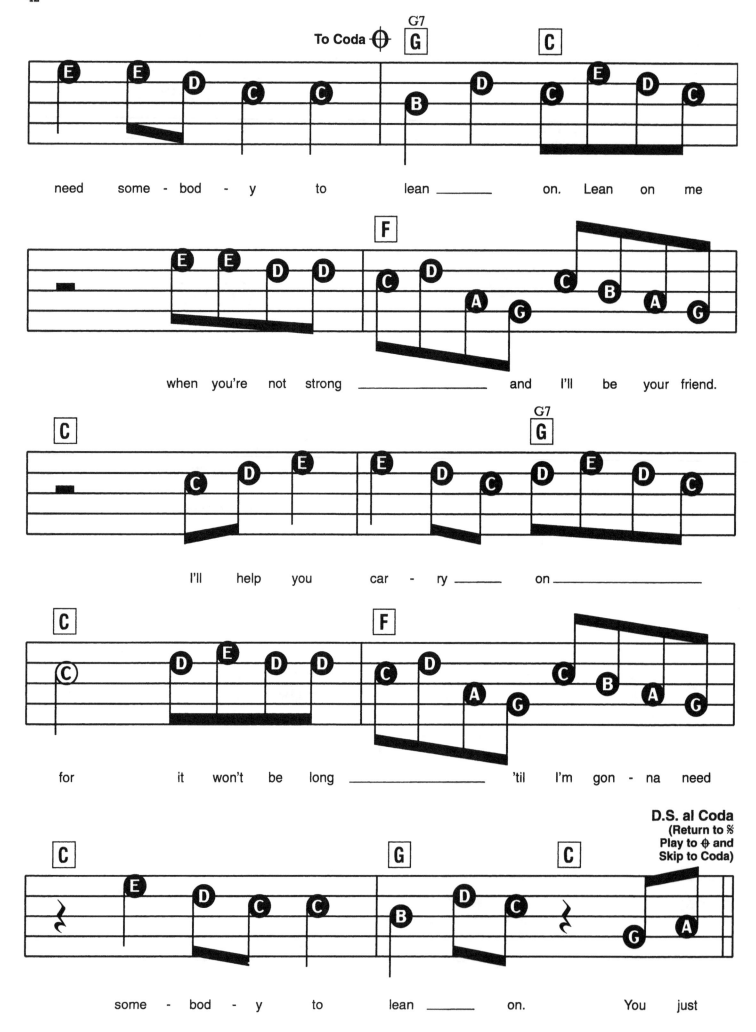

43

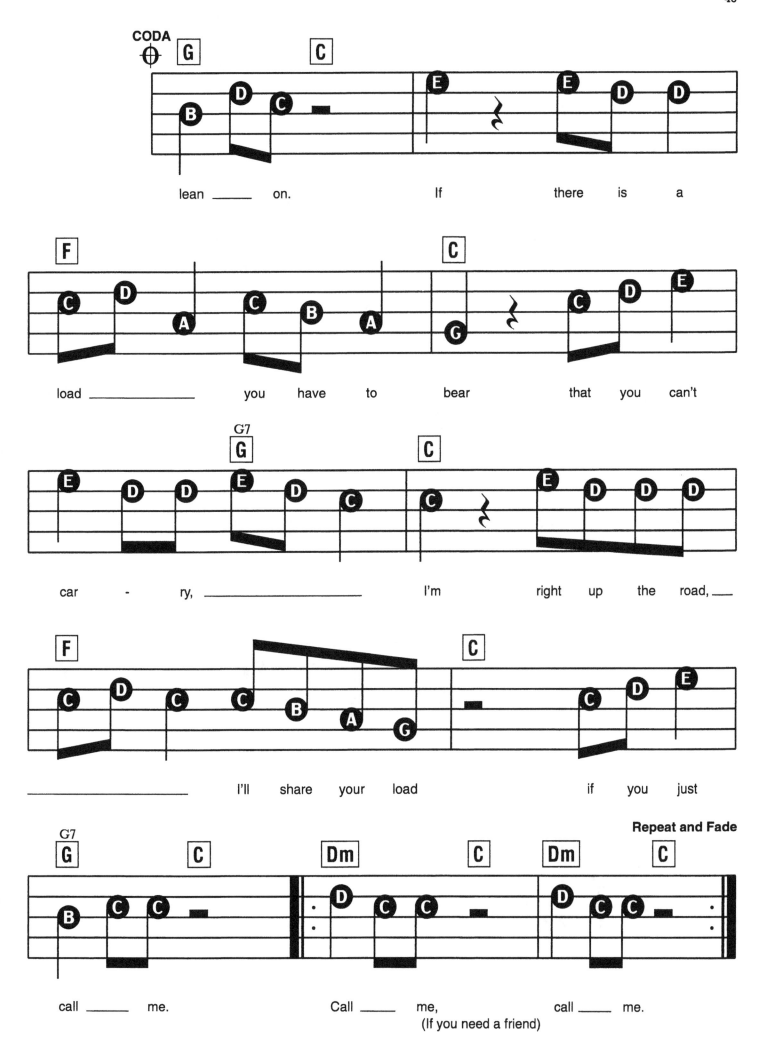

Hello Mudduh, Hello Fadduh!
(A Letter from Camp)

Registration 9
Rhythm: March

Words by Allan Sherman
Music by Lou Busch

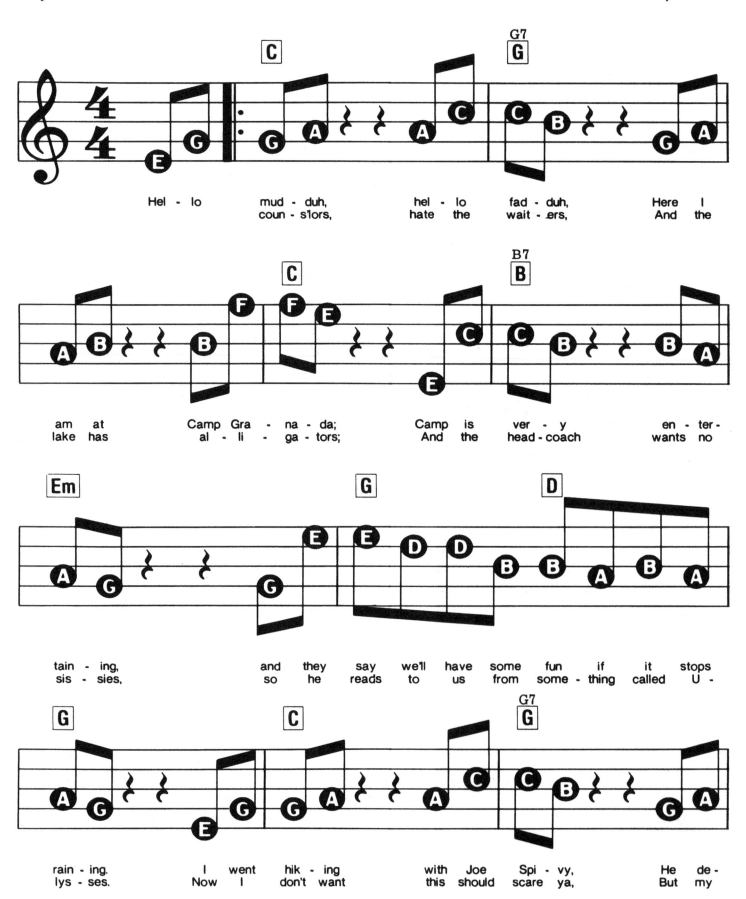

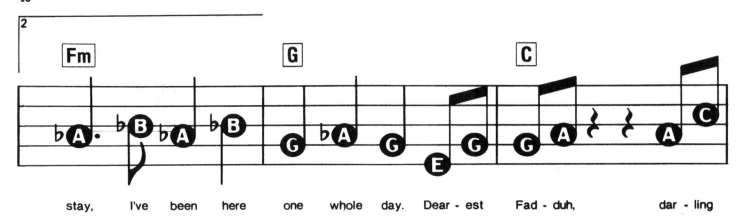

stay, I've been here one whole day. Dear - est Fad - duh, dar - ling

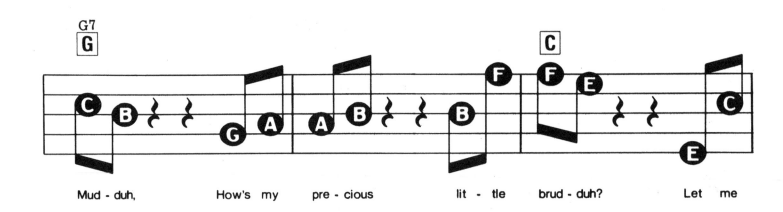

Mud - duh, How's my pre - cious lit - tle brud - duh? Let me

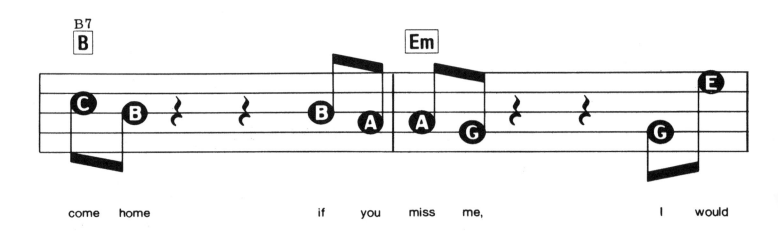

come home if you miss me, I would

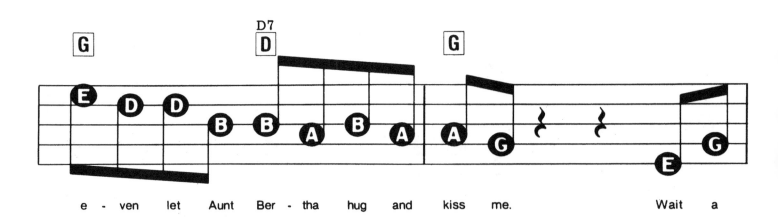

e - ven let Aunt Ber - tha hug and kiss me. Wait a

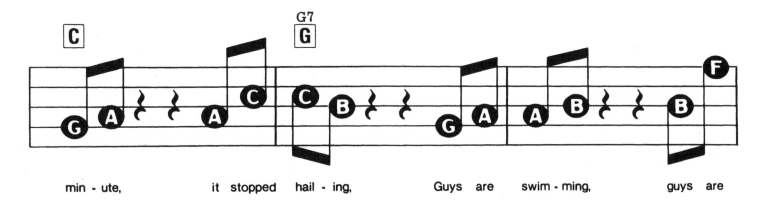

min - ute,   it stopped hail - ing,   Guys are swim - ming,   guys are

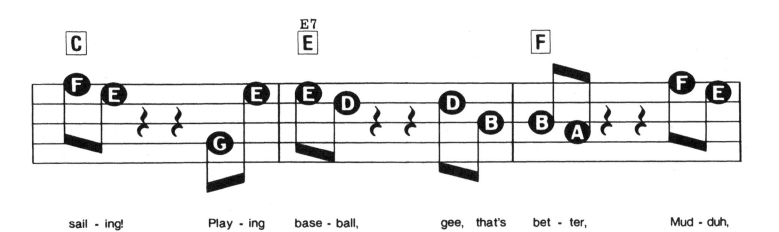

sail - ing!   Play - ing base - ball,   gee, that's bet - ter,   Mud - duh,

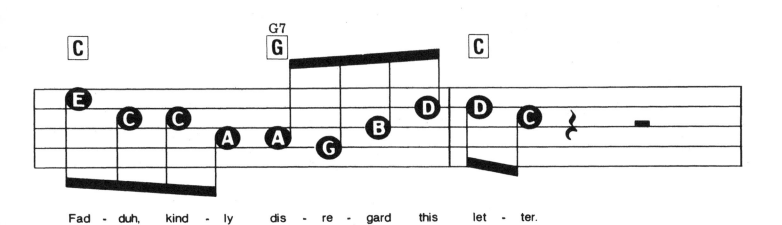

Fad - duh, kind - ly dis - re - gard this let - ter.

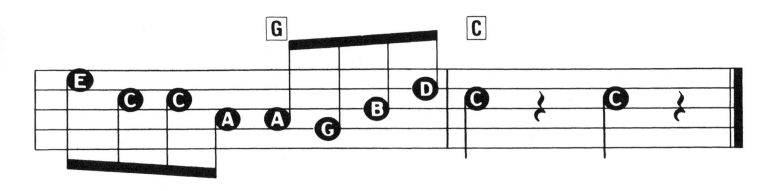

The House of the Rising Sun

Registration 4
Rhythm: Waltz

Words and Music by
Alan Price

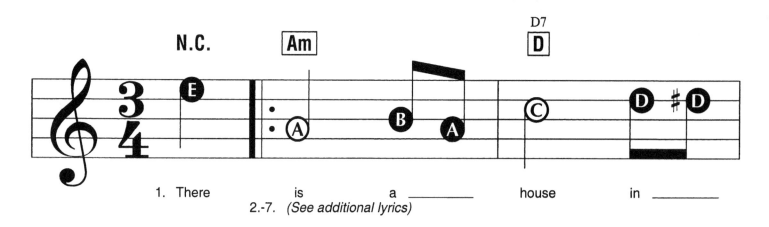

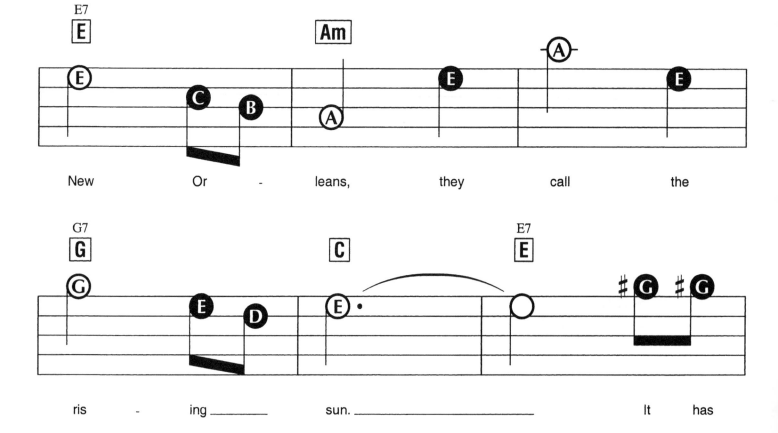

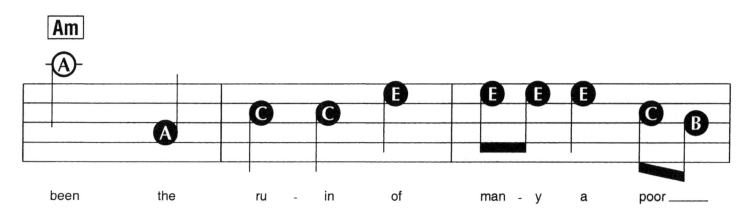

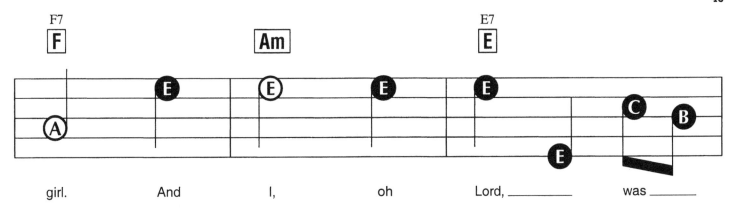

girl.   And   I,   oh   Lord,_____   was_____

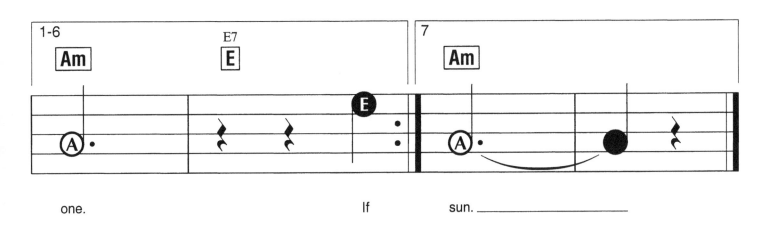

one.   If   sun._____

Additional Lyrics

2. If I had listened to what mama said,
   I'd 'a' been at home today.
   Being so young and foolish, poor girl,
   Let a gambler lead me astray.

3. My mother, she's a tailor,
   She sells those new blue jeans.
   My sweetheart, he's a drunkard, Lord,
   Drinks down in New Orleans.

4. The only thing a drunkard needs
   Is a suitcase and a trunk.
   The only time he's satisfied
   Is when he's on a drunk.

5. Go tell my baby, sister,
   Never do like I have done.
   To shun that house in New Orleans,
   They call the Rising Sun.

6. One foot is on the platform,
   And the other one on the train.
   I'm going back to New Orleans
   To wear that ball and chain.

7. I'm going back to New Orleans,
   My race is almost run.
   Going back to end my life
   Beneath the rising sun.

I Walk the Line

Registration 8
Rhythm: Country or Ballad

Words and Music by
John R. Cash

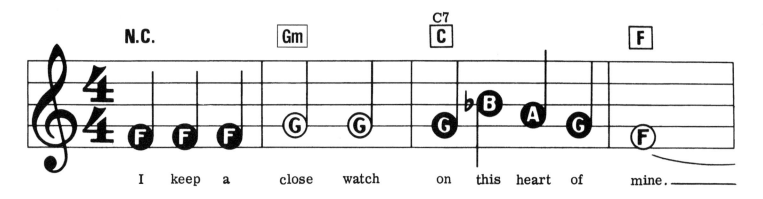

I keep a close watch on this heart of mine.

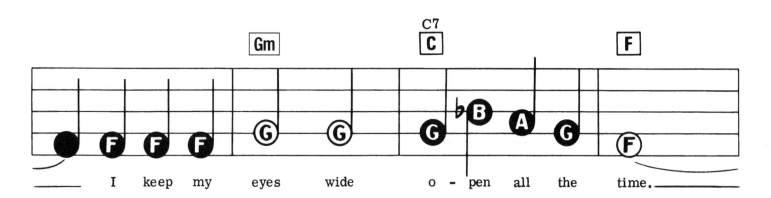

I keep my eyes wide o - pen all the time.

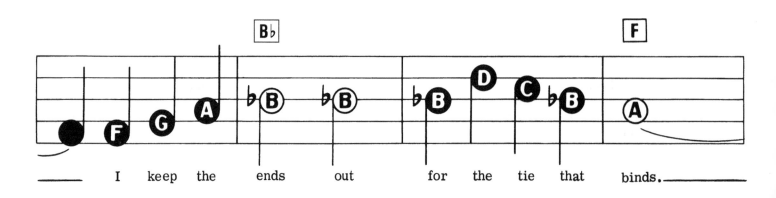

I keep the ends out for the tie that binds.

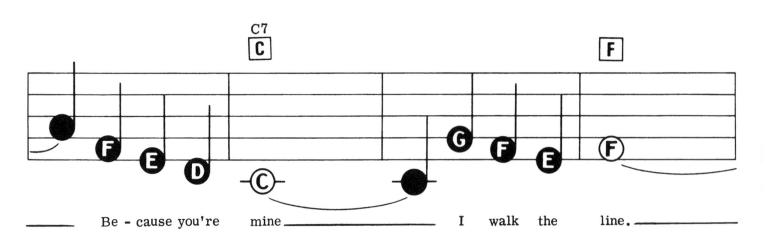

Be - cause you're mine I walk the line.

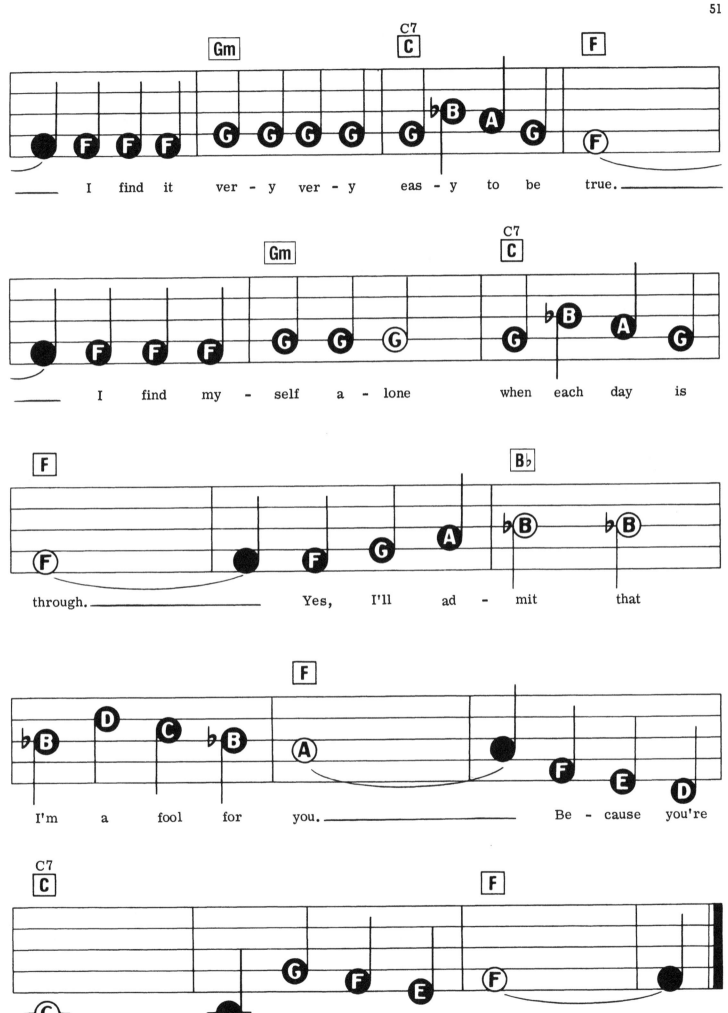

I'd Like to Teach the World to Sing

Registration 4
Rhythm: Rock

Words and Music by Bill Backer,
Roquel Davis, Roger Cook
and Roger Greenaway

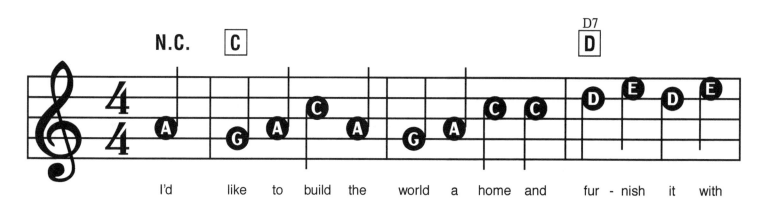

I'd   like   to   build   the   world   a   home   and   fur - nish   it   with

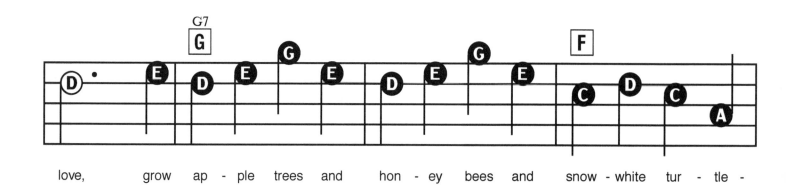

love,   grow   ap - ple   trees   and   hon - ey   bees   and   snow - white   tur - tle -

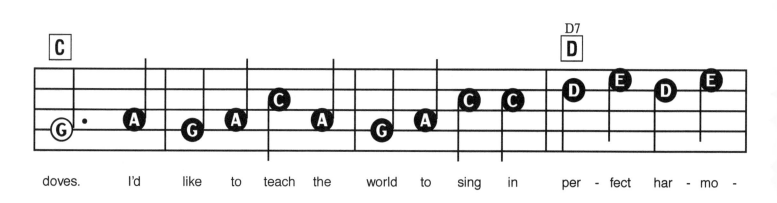

doves.   I'd   like   to   teach   the   world   to   sing   in   per - fect   har - mo -

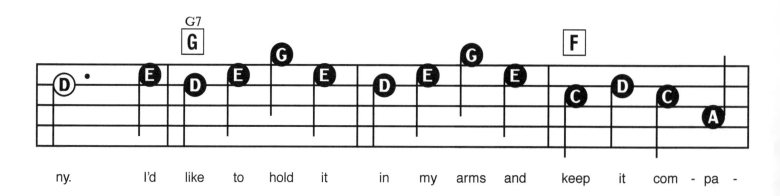

ny.   I'd   like   to   hold   it   in   my   arms   and   keep   it   com - pa -

53

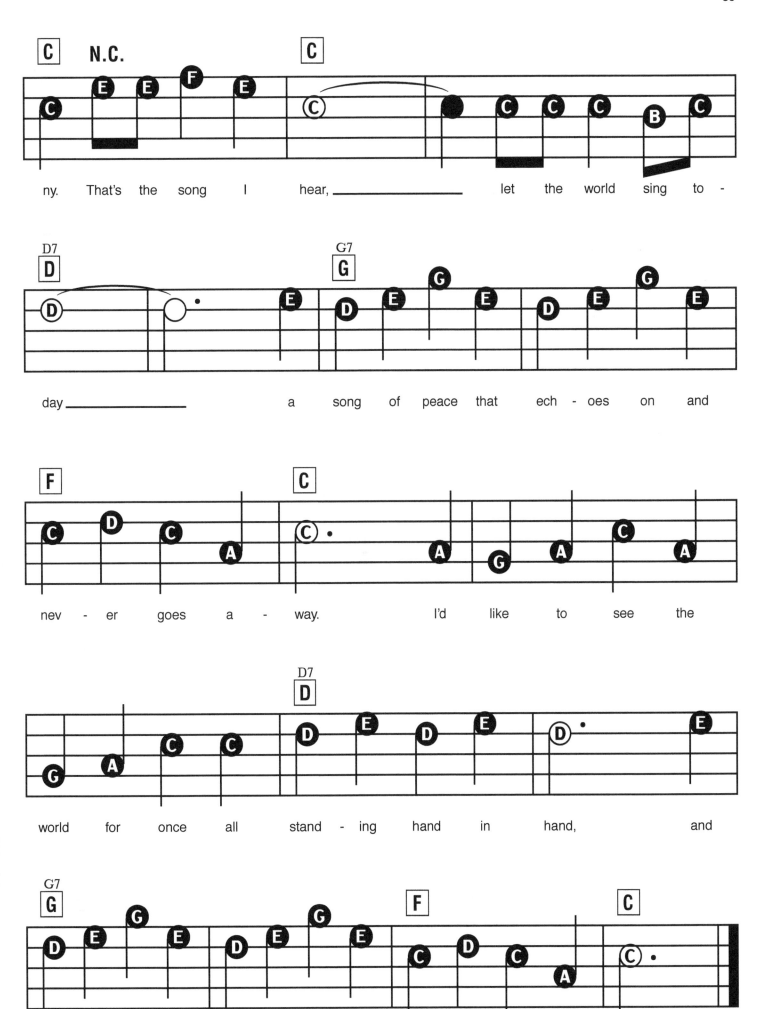

Leaving on a Jet Plane

Registration 1
Rhythm: Rock or Slow Rock

Words and Music by
John Denver

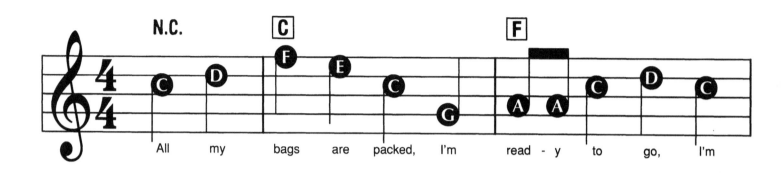

All my bags are packed, I'm read-y to go, I'm

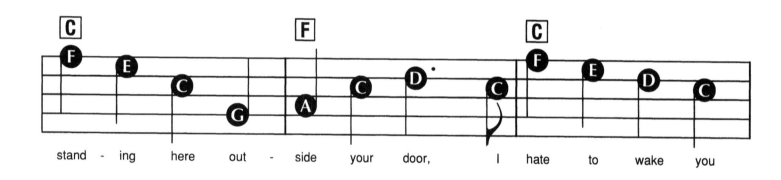

stand - ing here out - side your door, I hate to wake you

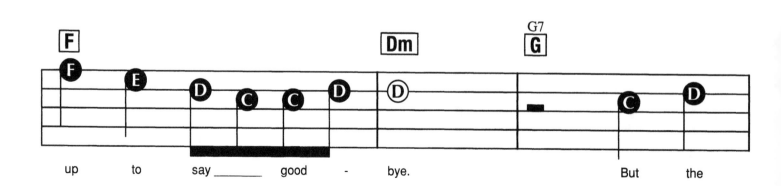

up to say _____ good - bye. But the

55

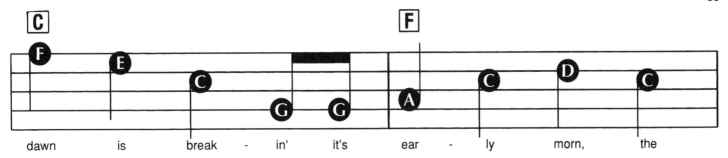

dawn   is   break - in'   it's   ear - ly   morn,   the

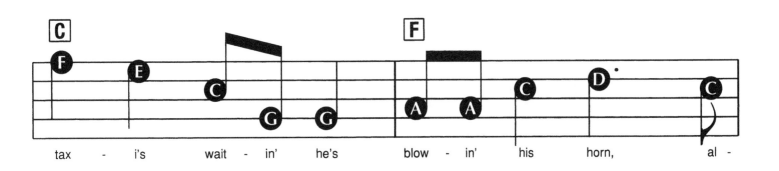

tax - i's   wait - in'   he's   blow - in'   his   horn,   al -

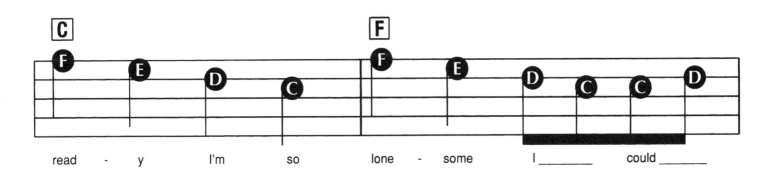

read - y   I'm   so   lone - some   I_____   could_____

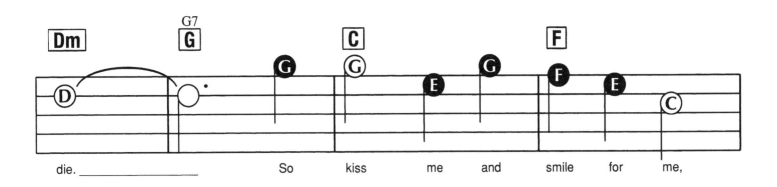

die._____   So   kiss   me   and   smile   for   me,

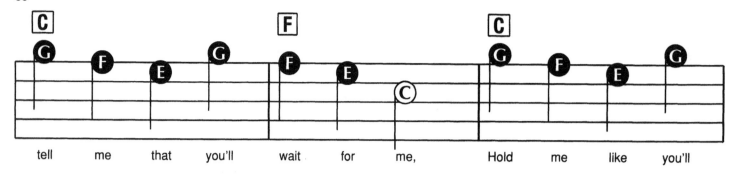

tell   me   that   you'll   wait   for   me,   Hold   me   like   you'll

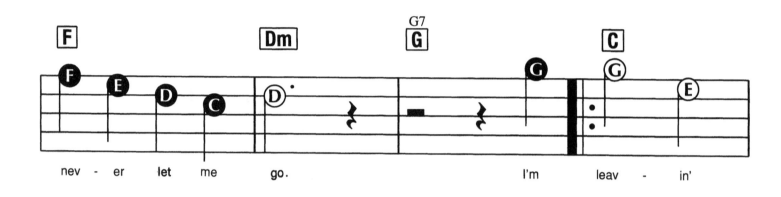

nev - er   let   me   go.   I'm   leav - in'

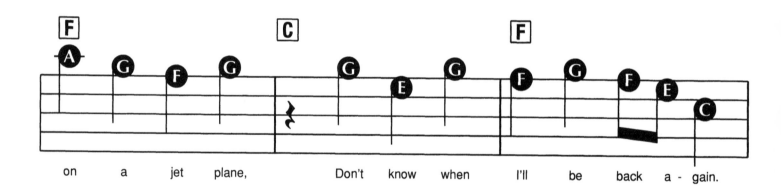

on   a   jet   plane,   Don't   know   when   I'll   be   back   a - gain.

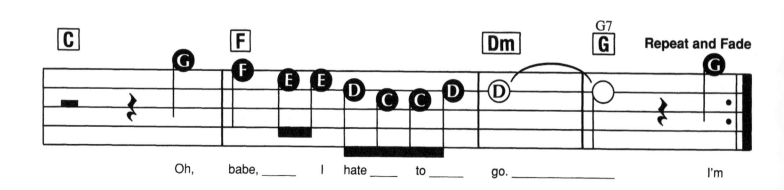

Oh,   babe, _____   I   hate ____ to _____ go. _____   I'm

Sundown

Registration 4
Rhythm: Rock or Slow Rock

Words and Music by
Gordon Lightfoot

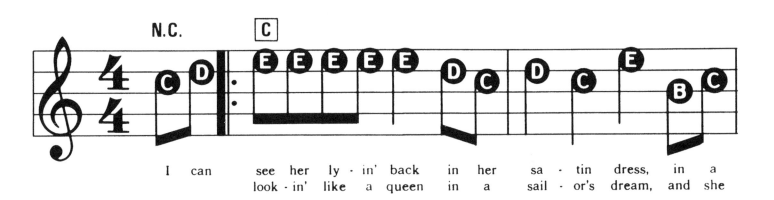

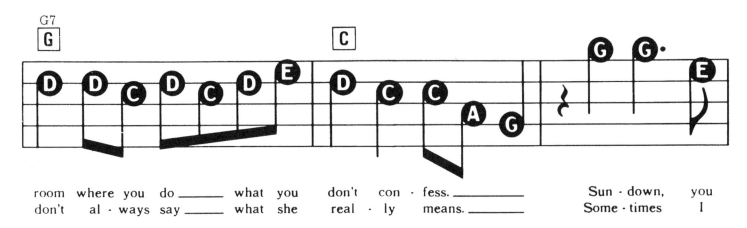

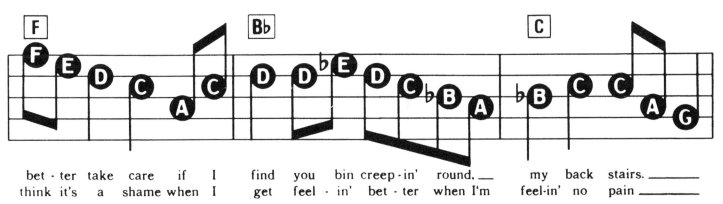

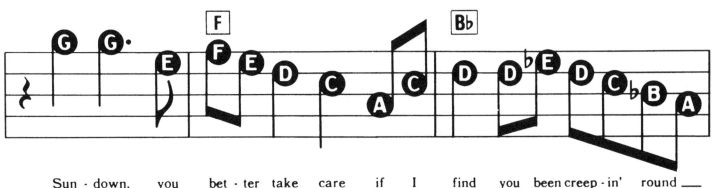

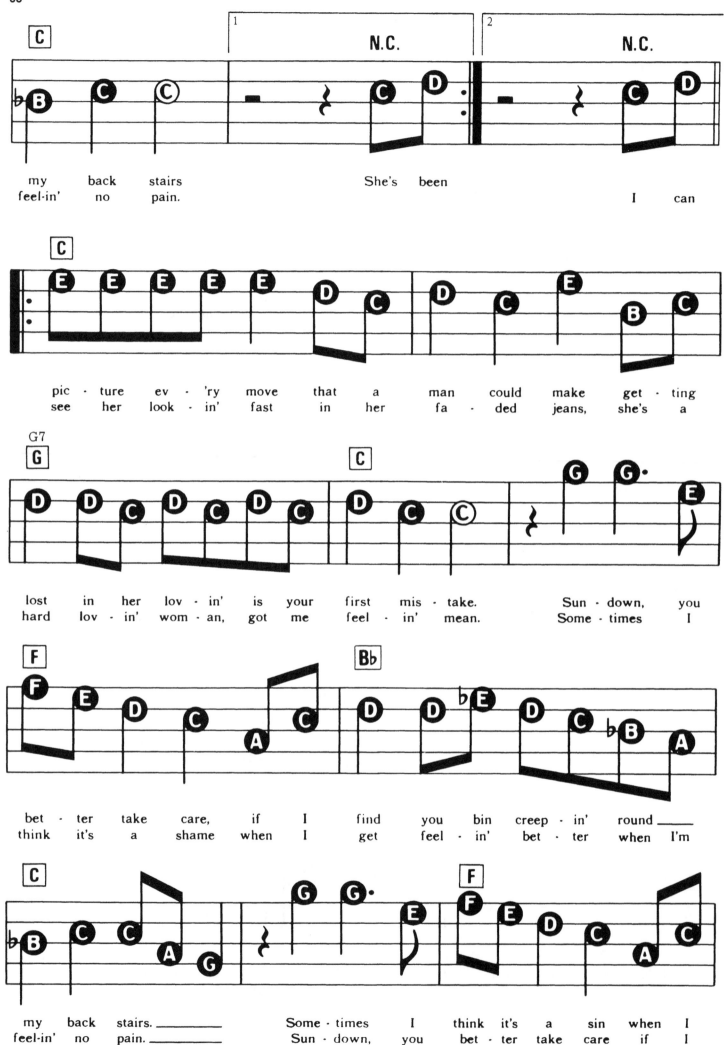

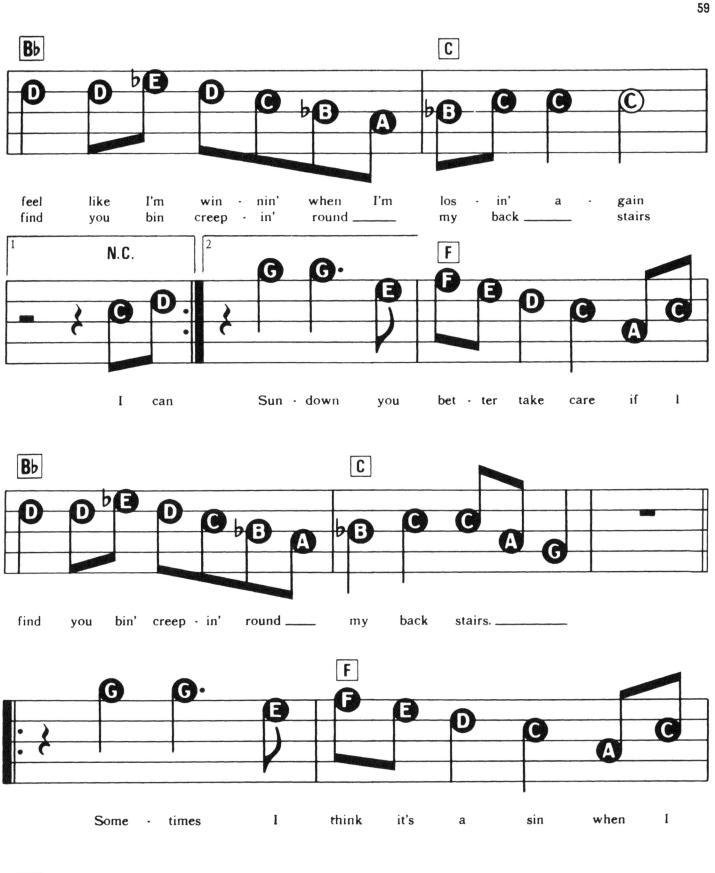

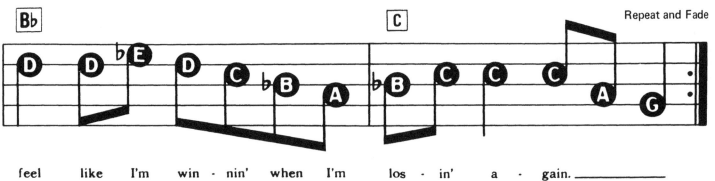

Let It Be

Registration 3
Rhythm: Rock or Ballad

Words and Music by John Lennon
and Paul McCartney

When I find my-self in times of trou-ble, Moth-er Mar-y
when the bro-ken - heart-ed peo-ple liv-ing in the

comes to me, speak - ing words of wis - dom, let it
world a - gree there will be an an - swer, let it

be. _____ And in my hour of dark - ness she is
be. _____ For though they may be part - ed, there is

stand - ing right in front of me, speak - ing words of
still a chance that they may see, there will be an

wis - dom, let it be. _____ Let it
an - swer, let it be. _____ Let it

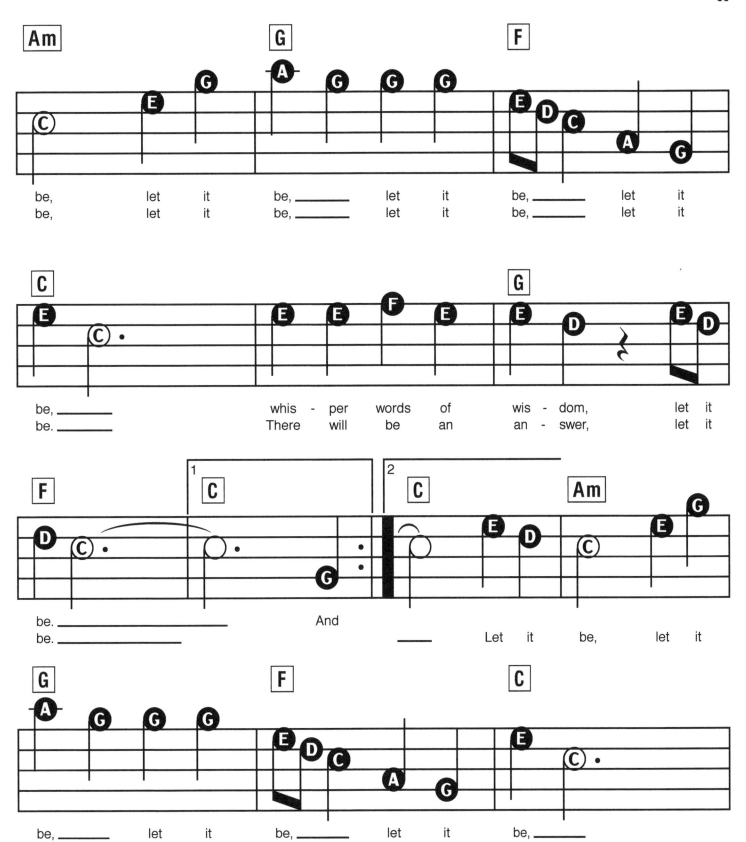

be,   let it   be, _____ let it   be, _____ let it
be,   let it   be, _____ let it   be, _____ let it

be, _____   whis - per words of   wis - dom,   let it
be. _____   There will be an   an - swer,   let it

be. _____   And
be. _____   _____ Let it be,   let it

be, _____ let it   be, _____ let it   be, _____

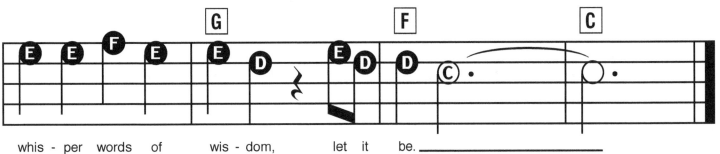

whis - per words of   wis - dom,   let it be. _____

The Lion Sleeps Tonight

Registration 7
Rhythm: Rock or Swing

New Lyrics and Revised Music by George David Weiss,
Hugo Peretti and Luigi Creatore

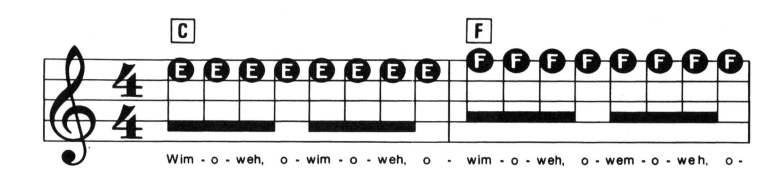

Wim - o - weh, o - wim - o - weh, o - wim - o - weh, o - wem - o - weh, o -

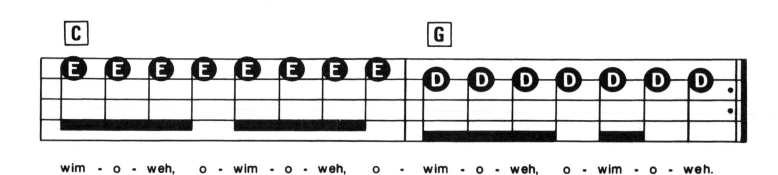

wim - o - weh, o - wim - o - weh, o - wim - o - weh, o - wim - o - weh.

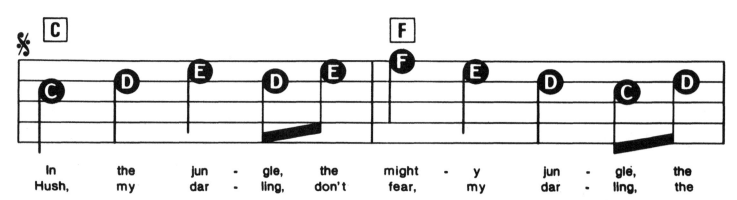

In the jun - gle, the might - y jun - gle, the
Hush, my dar - ling, don't fear, my dar - ling, the

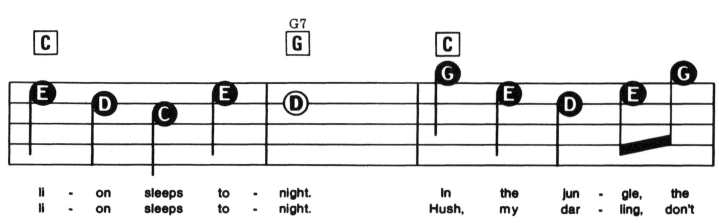

li - on sleeps to - night. In the jun - gle, the
li - on sleeps to - night. Hush, my dar - ling, don't

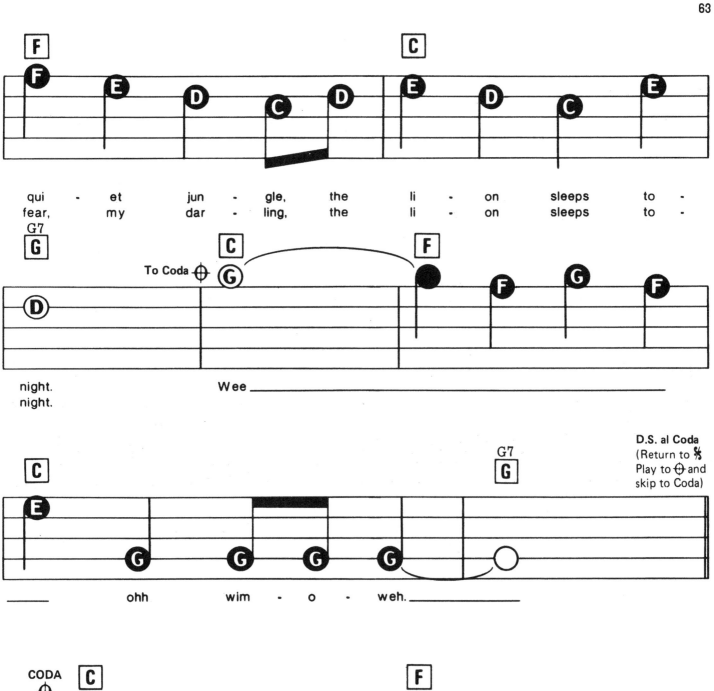

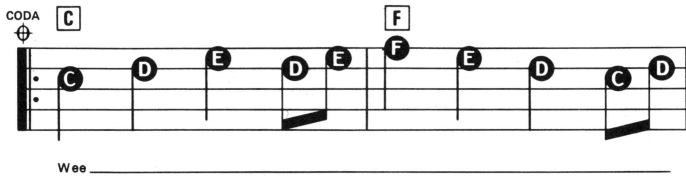

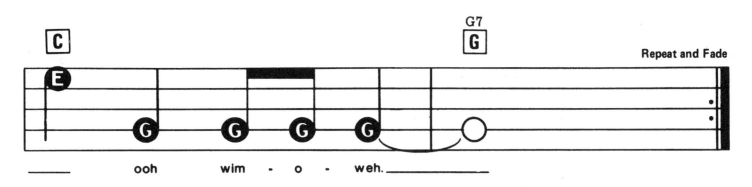

Mountain Dew

Registration 8
Rhythm: Country or Fox Trot

Words and Music by Scott Wiseman
and Bascomb Lunsford

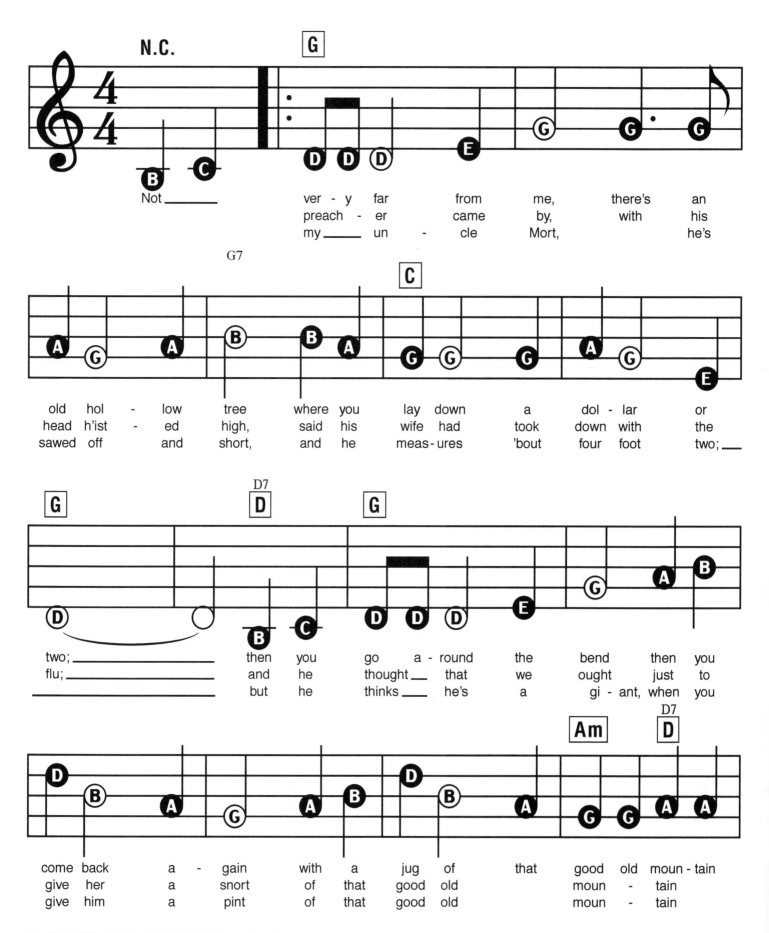

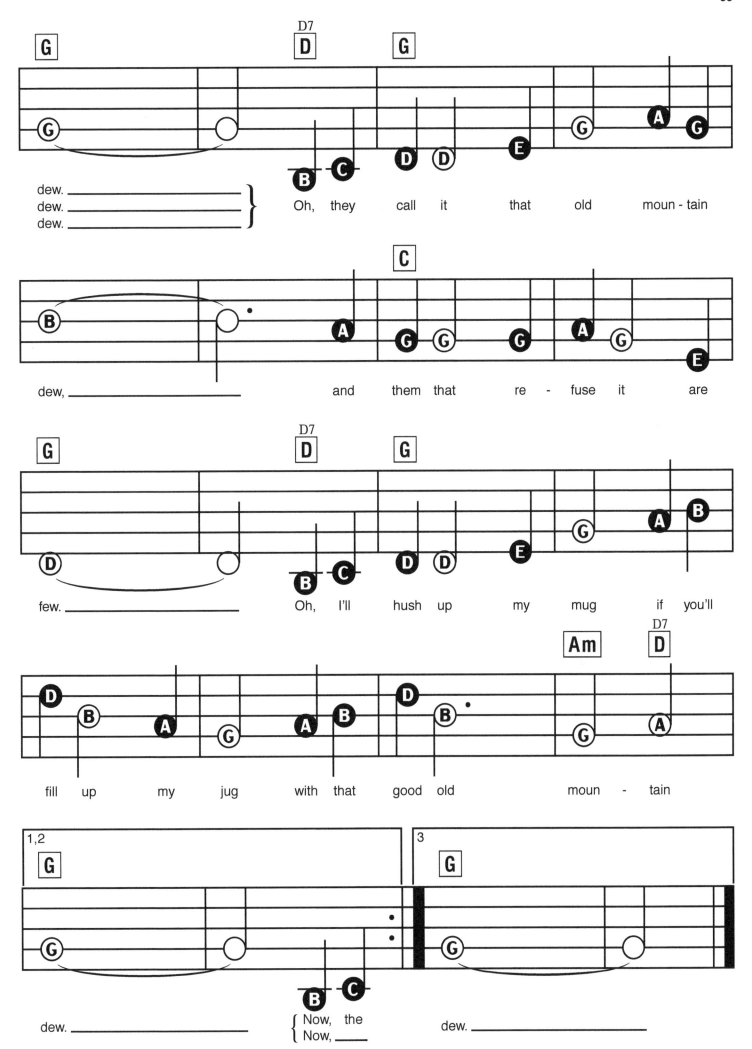

On Top of Spaghetti

Registration 2
Rhythm: Waltz

Words and Music by
Tom Glazer

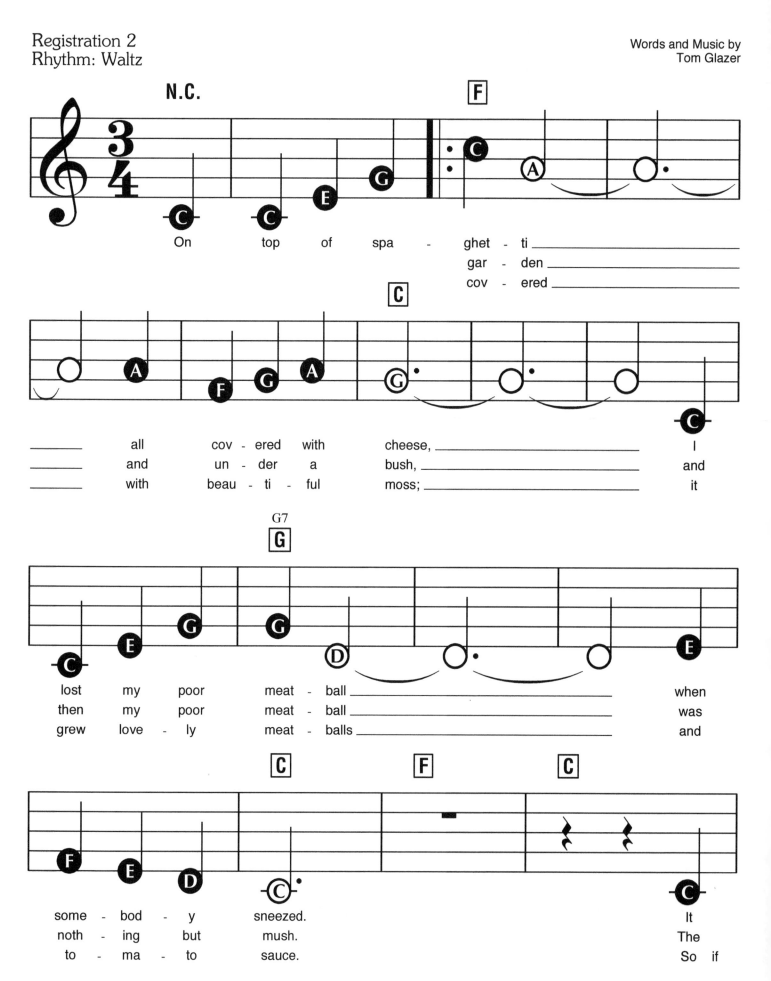

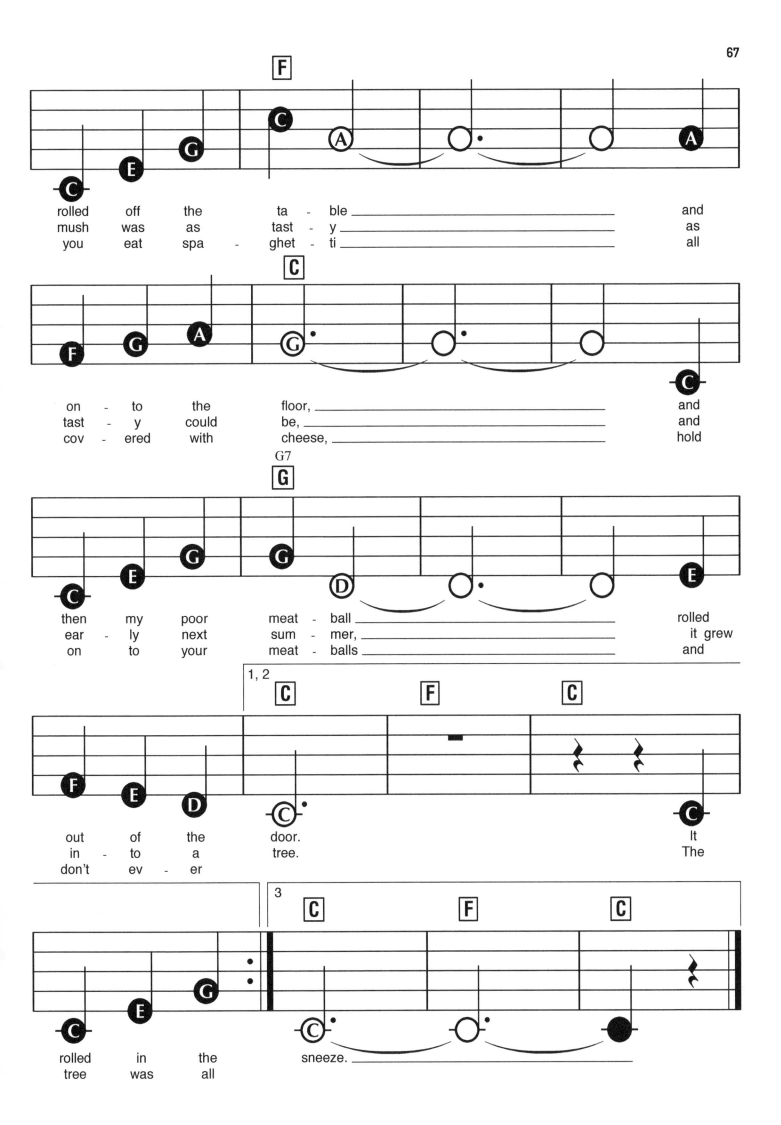

Peaceful Easy Feeling

Registration 4
Rhythm: Soft Rock

Words and Music by
Jack Tempchin

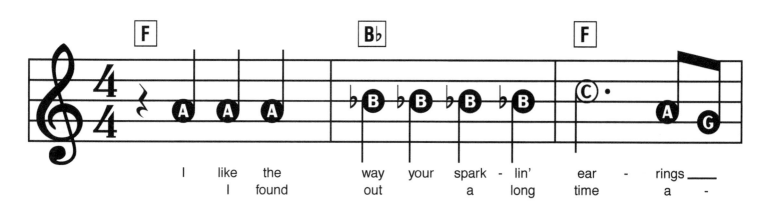

I like the way your spark - lin' ear - rings ____
I found out a long time a -

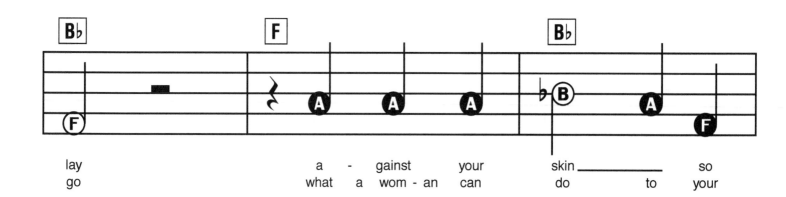

lay a - gainst your skin ____ so
go what a wom - an can do to your

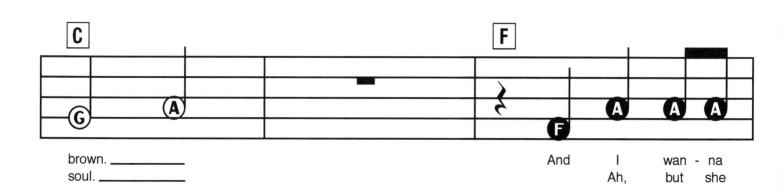

brown. ____
soul. ____

And I wan - na
Ah, but she

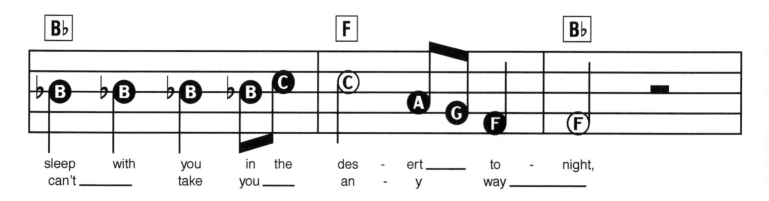

sleep with you in the des - ert ____ to - night,
can't ____ take you ____ an - y way ____

69

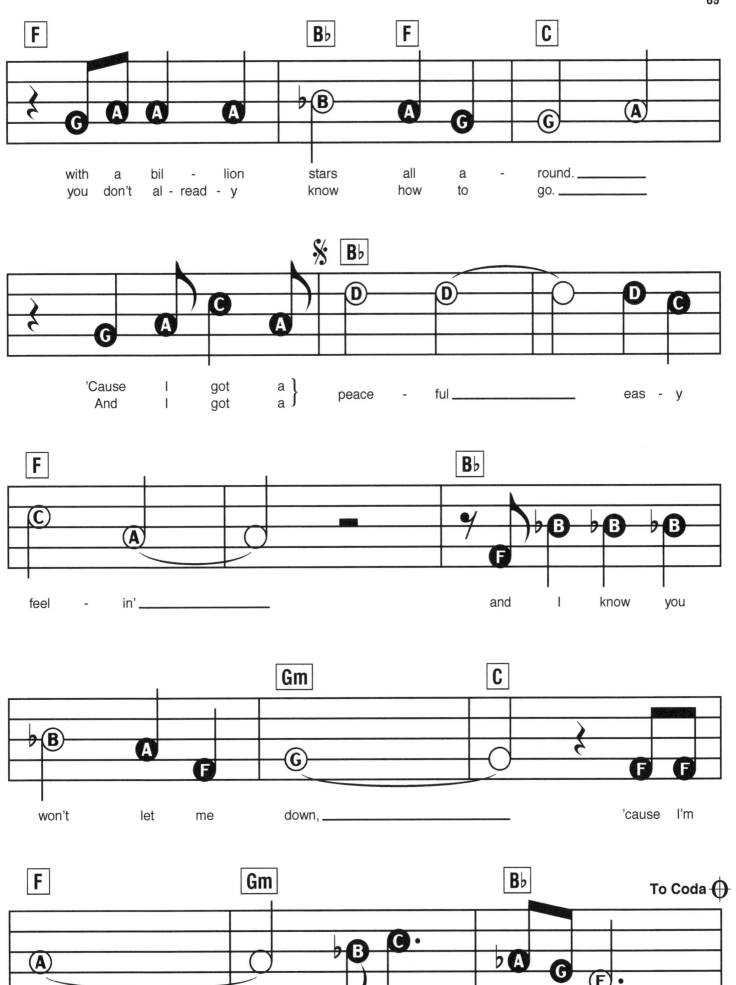

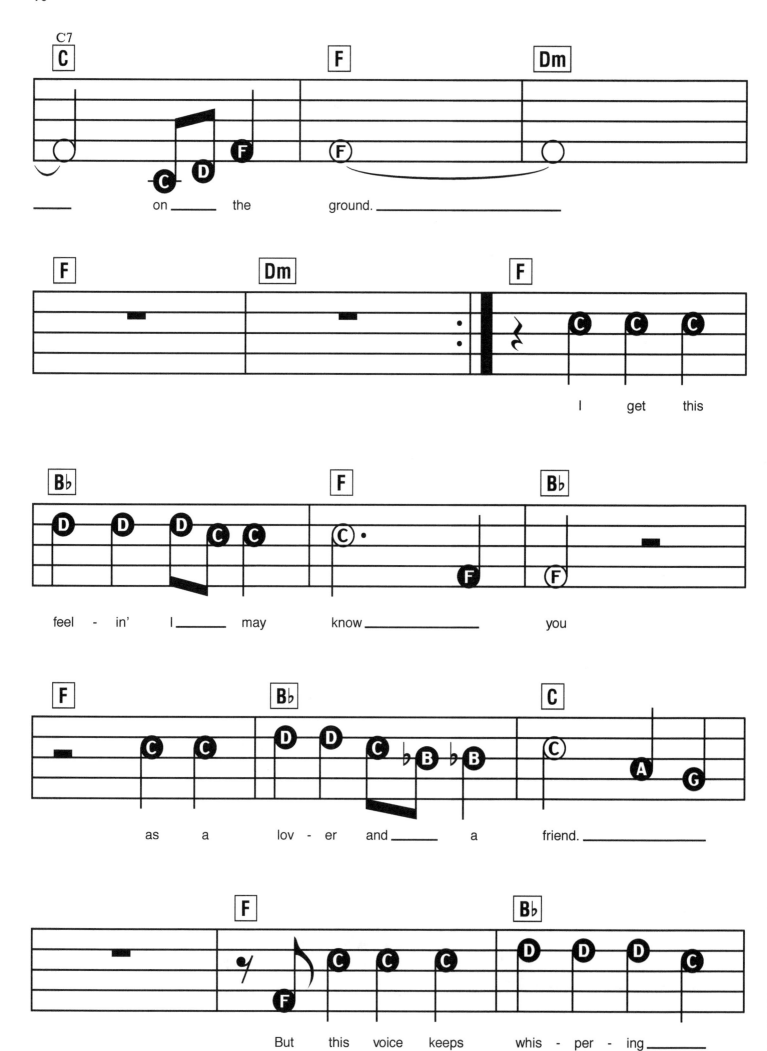

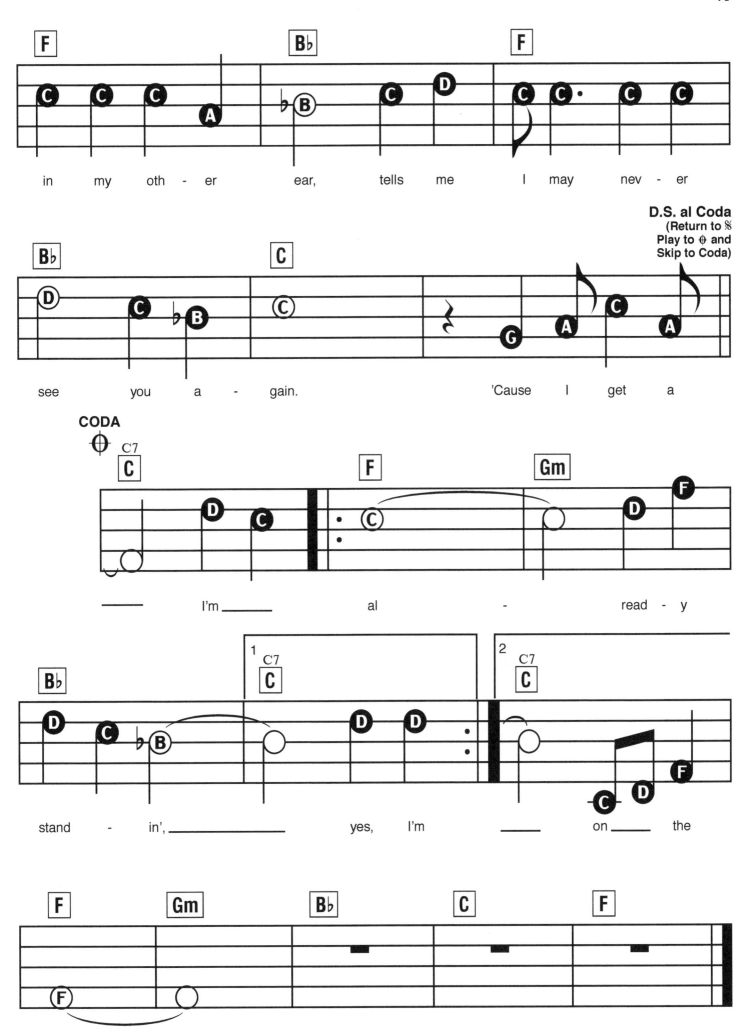

Puff the Magic Dragon

Registration 2
Rhythm: Swing

Words and Music by Lenny Lipton and
Peter Yarrow

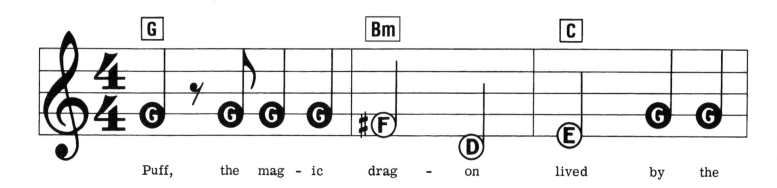

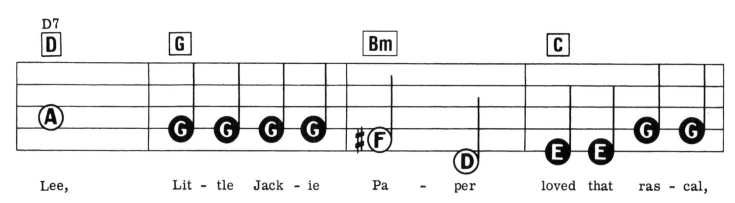

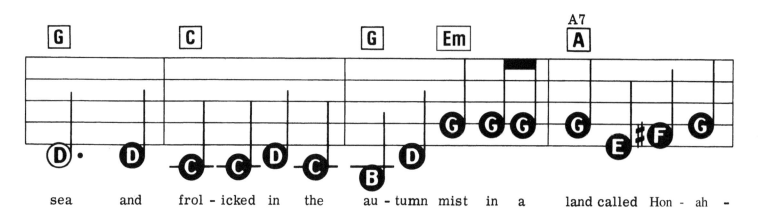

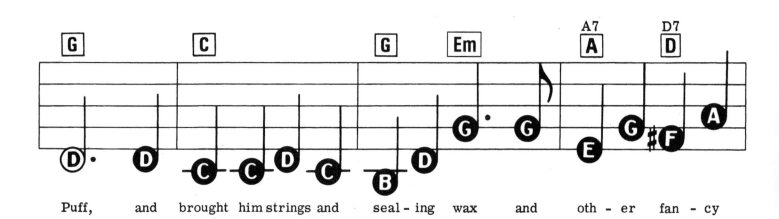

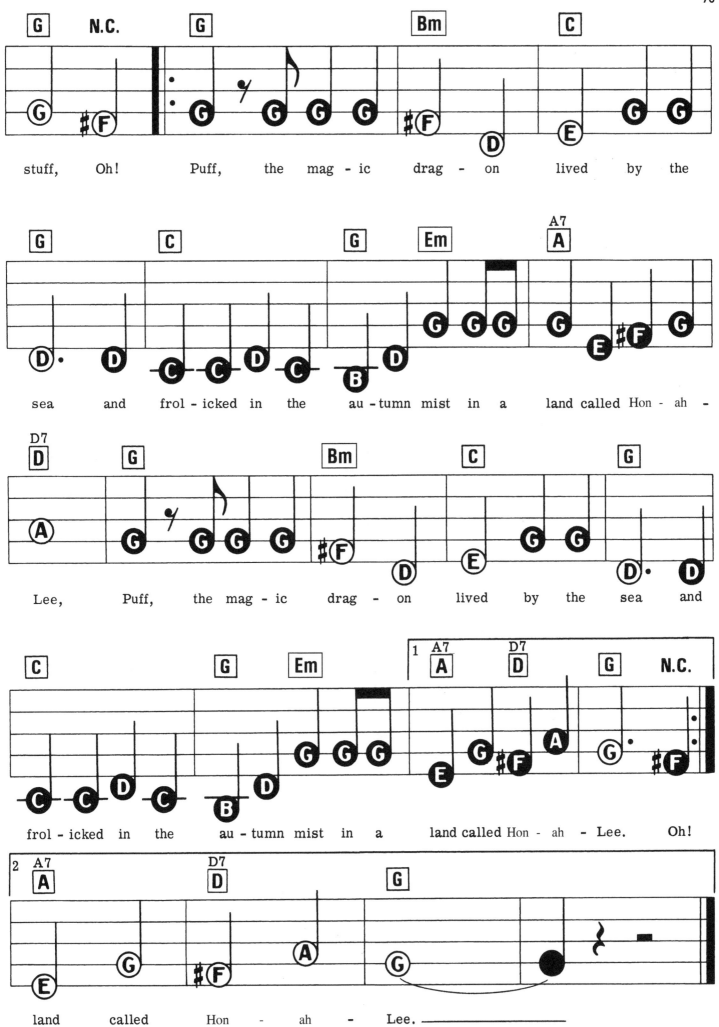

Take Me Home, Country Roads

Registration 10
Rhythm: Country

Words and Music by John Denver,
Bill Danoff and Taffy Nivert

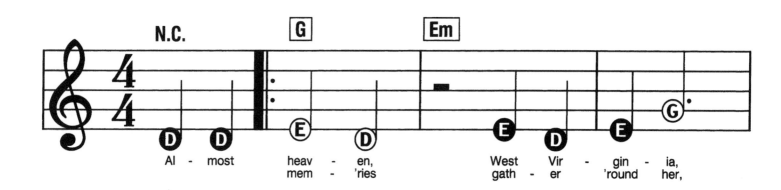

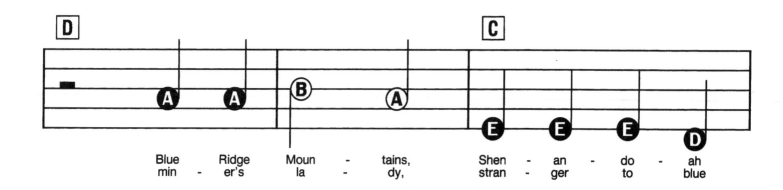

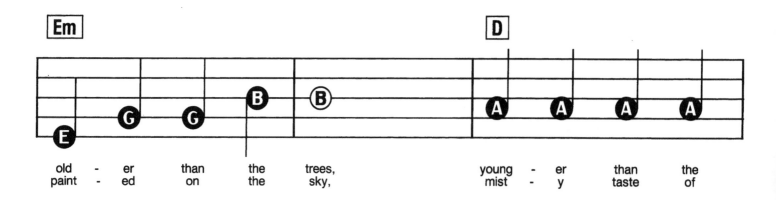

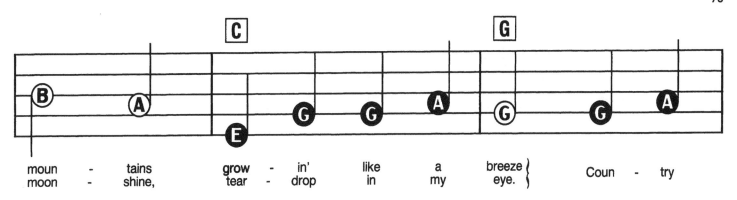

moun - tains grow - in' like a breeze
moon - shine, tear - drop in my eye. } Coun - try

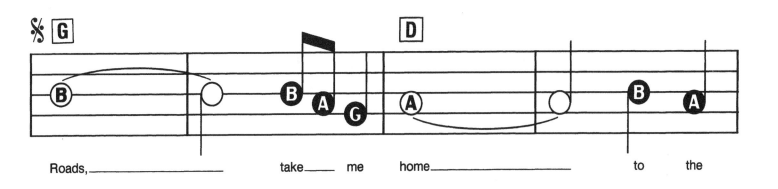

Roads,_____ take__ me home_____ to the

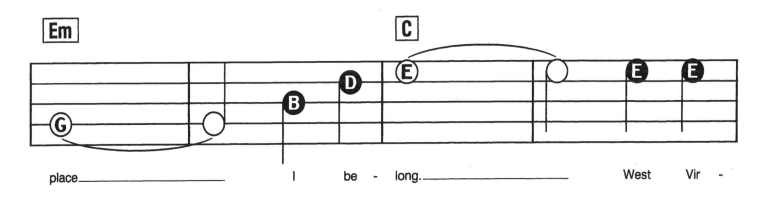

place_____ I be - long._____ West Vir -

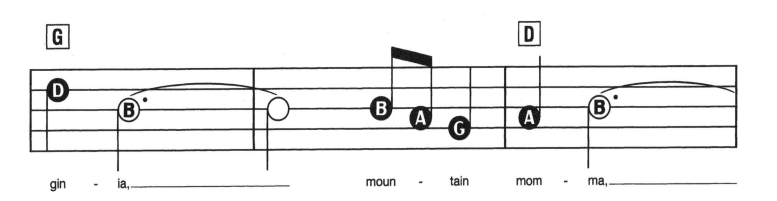

gin - ia,_____ moun - tain mom - ma,_____

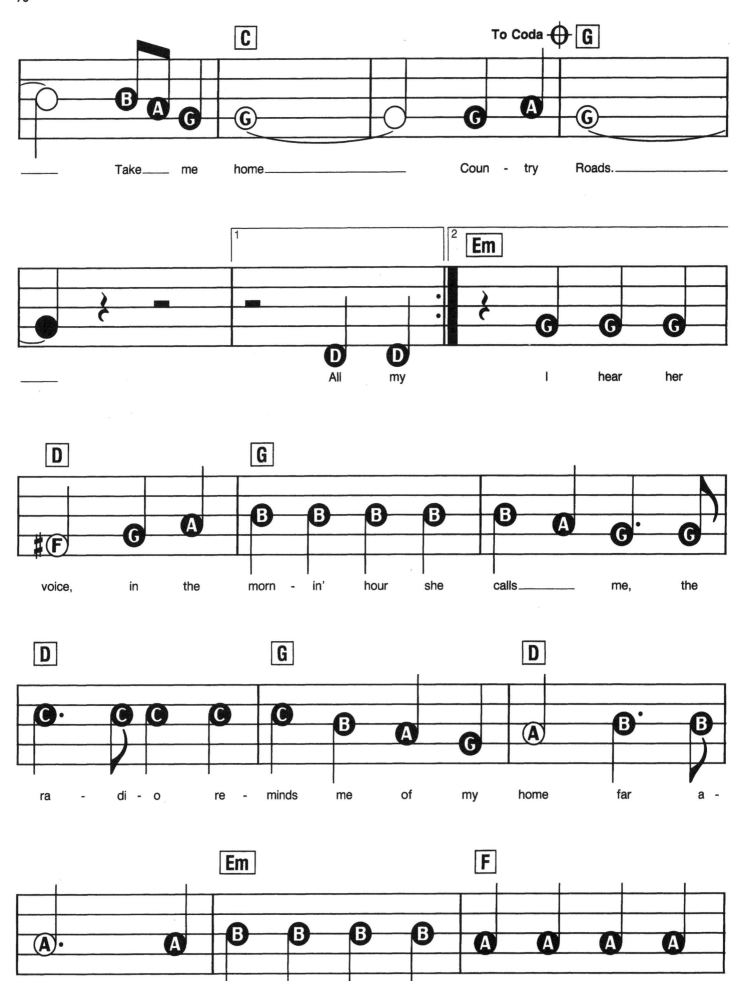

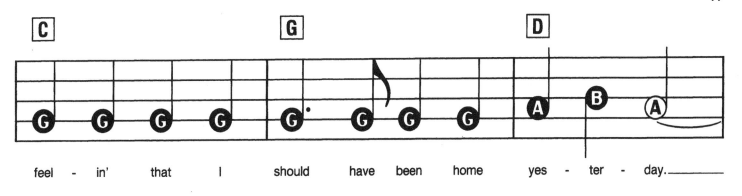

feel - in' that I should have been home yes - ter - day.

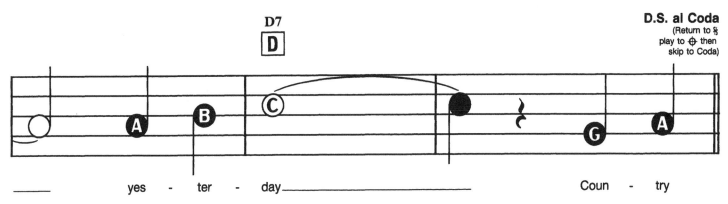

D.S. al Coda
(Return to %
play to ⊕ then
skip to Coda)

___ yes - ter - day ___ Coun - try

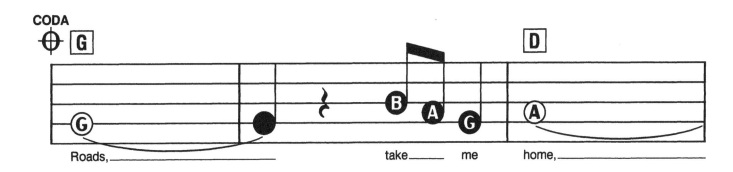

CODA

Roads, ___ take ___ me home,

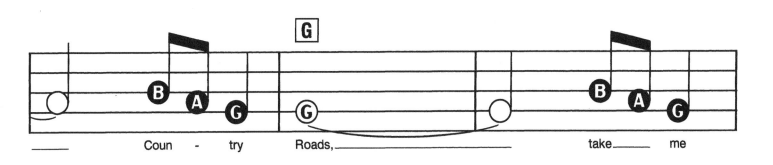

___ Coun - try Roads, ___ take ___ me

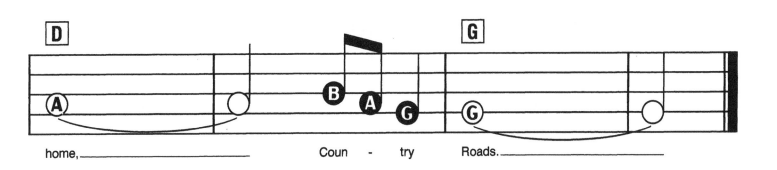

home, ___ Coun - try Roads. ___

This Land Is Your Land

Registration 9
Rhythm: Country or Swing

Words and Music by
Woody Guthrie

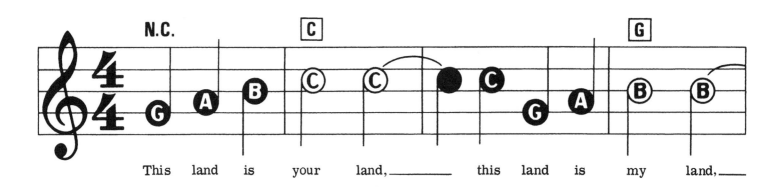

This land is your land, _____ this land is my land, _____

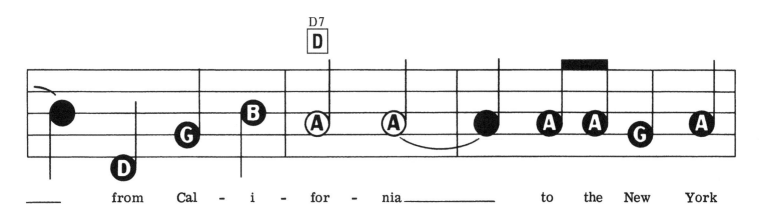

_____ from Cal - i - for - nia _____ to the New York

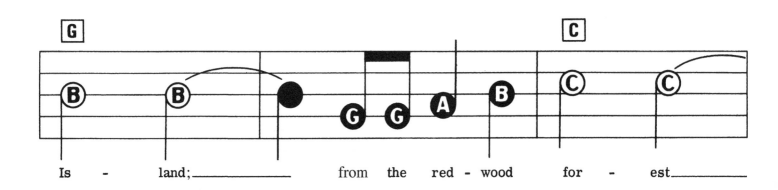

Is - land; _____ from the red - wood for - est _____

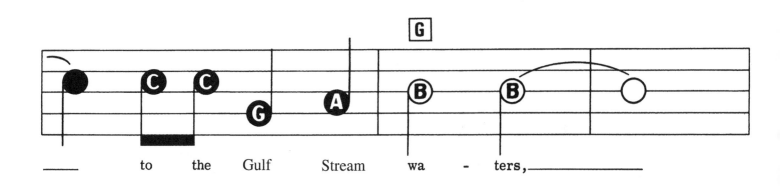

_____ to the Gulf Stream wa - ters, _____

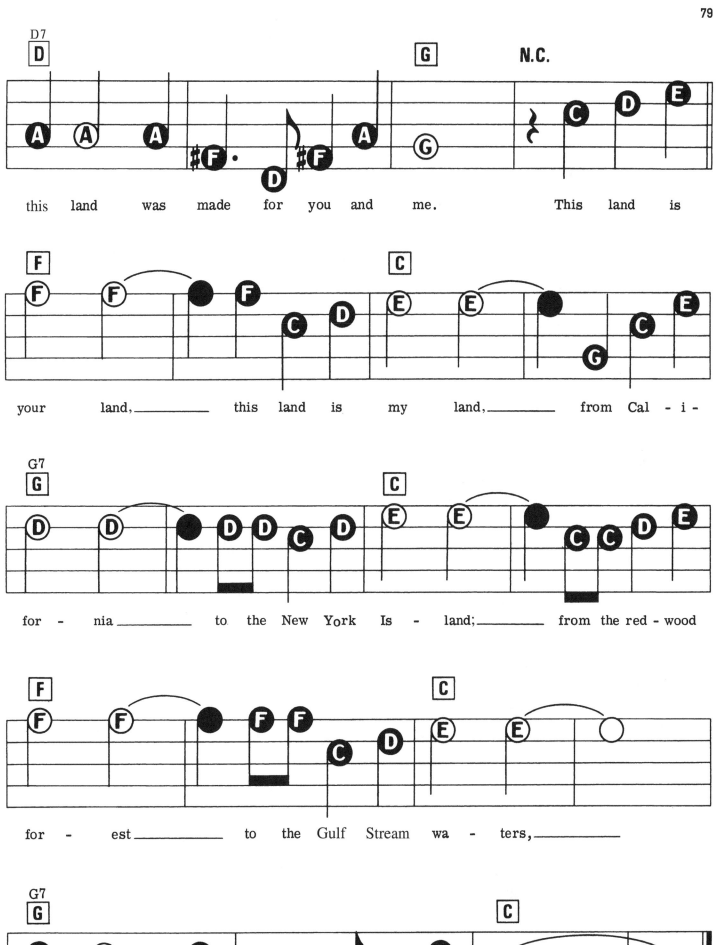

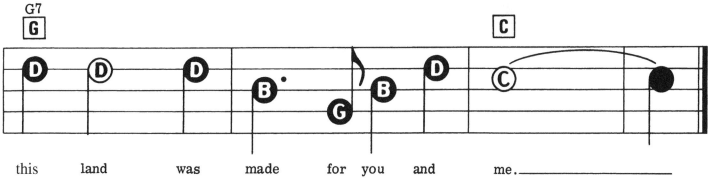

Tie Me Kangaroo Down Sport

Registration 2
Rhythm: Fox Trot or Swing

Words and Music by
Rolf Harris

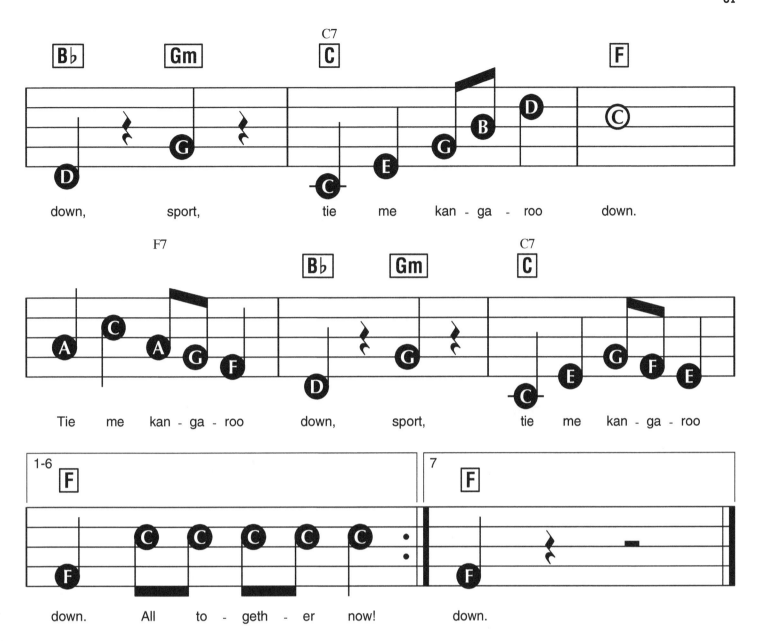

down,   sport,   tie   me   kan - ga - roo   down.

Tie   me   kan - ga - roo   down,   sport,   tie   me   kan - ga - roo

down.   All   to - geth - er   now!   down.

Additional Lyrics

2. Keep me cockatoo cool, Curl,
   Keep me cockatoo cool.
   Don't go acting the fool, Curl,
   Just keep me cockatoo cool...
   All together now!
   Chorus

3. Take me koala back, Jack,
   Take me koala back.
   He lives somewhere out on the track, Mac,
   So take me koala back.
   All together now!
   Chorus

4. Let me abos go loose, Lew,
   Let me abos go loose.
   They're of no further use, Lew,
   So let me abos go loose.
   All together now!
   Chorus

5. Mind me platypus duck, Bill,
   Mind me platypus duck.
   Don't let him go running amok, Bill,
   Mind me platypus duck.
   All together now!
   Chorus

6. Play your didgeridoo, Blue,
   Play your didgeridoo.
   Keep playing 'til I shoot thro' Blue,
   Play your didgeridoo.
   All together now!
   Chorus

7. Tan me hide when I'm dead, Fred,
   Tan me hide when I'm dead.
   So we tanned his hide when he died, Clyde,
   (Spoken:) And that's it hanging on the shed.
   All together now!
   Chorus

The Unicorn

Registration 4
Rhythm: Folk or Swing

Words and Music by
Shel Silverstein

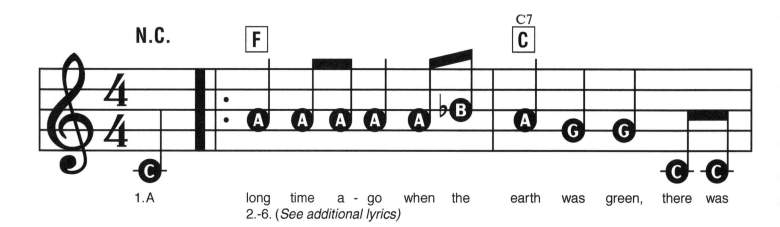

1.A long time a - go when the earth was green, there was
2.-6. (*See additional lyrics*)

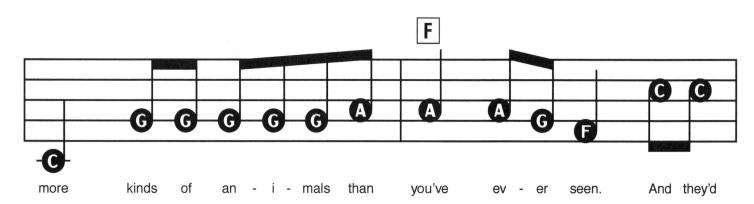

more kinds of an - i - mals than you've ev - er seen. And they'd

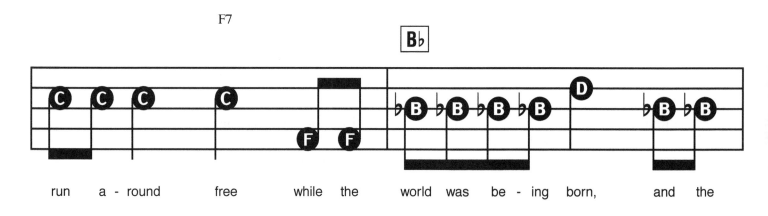

run a - round free while the world was be - ing born, and the

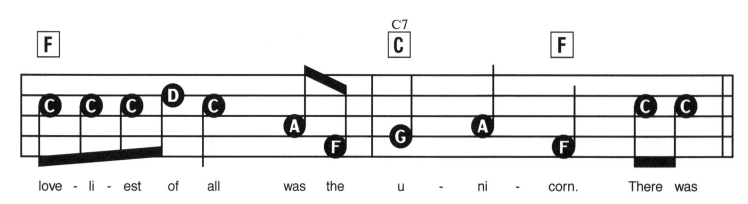

love - li - est of all was the u - ni - corn. There was

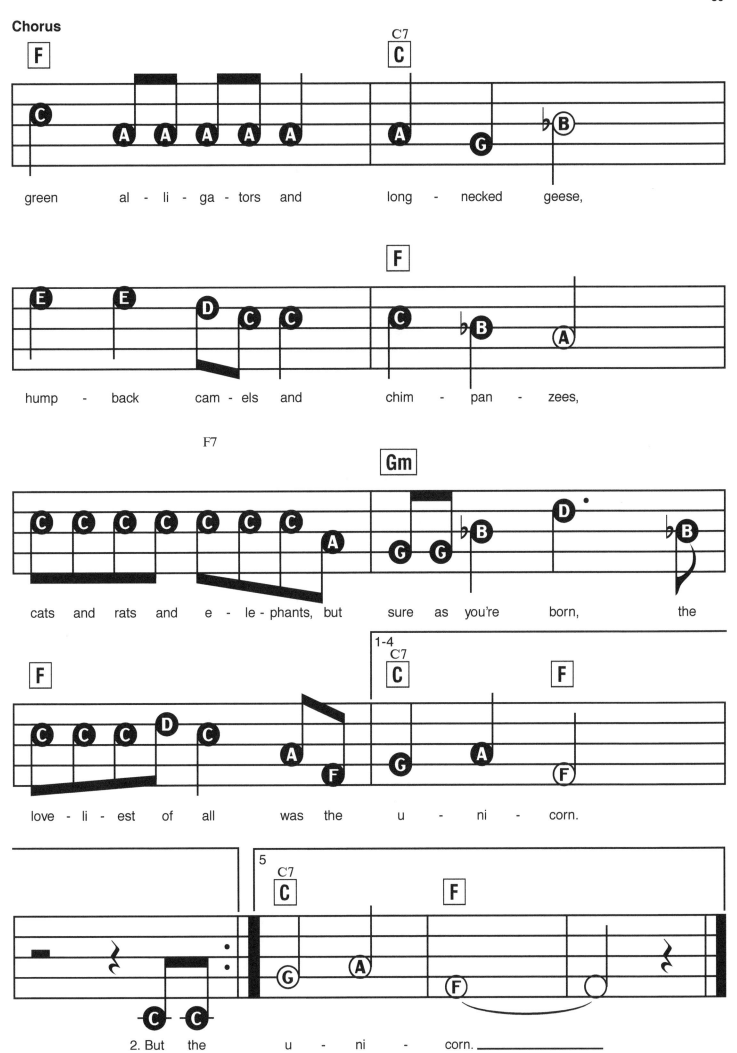

Additional Lyrics

2. But the Lord seen some sinnin' and it caused him pain.
   He says, "Stand back, I'm gonna make it rain."
   Says, "Hey, Brother Noah, I'll tell ya whatcha do.
   Go and build me a floatin' zoo."
   "And you take two alligators and a couple of geese,
Chorus: Two humpy bumpy camels and two chimpanzees.
   Take two cats and rats and elephants, but sure as you're born,
   Noah, don't you forget my unicorn."

3. Now Noah was there, he answered the callin'
   And he finished up the ark just as the rain started fallin'.
   He marched in the animals two by two,
   And called out as they went through,
Chorus: "Hey, Lord, I got your two alligators and your couple of geese,
   Your humpy bumpy camels and your chimpanzees.
   Got your cats and rats and elephants, but Lord, I'm so forlorn,
   'Cause I just don't see no unicorn."

4. Ol' Noah looked out through the drivin' rain,
   But the unicorns were hidin' – playin' silly games.
   They were kickin' and splashin' in the misty morn,
   Oh, them silly unicorn.
Chorus: "Hey, Lord, I got your two alligators and your couple of geese,
   Your humpy bumpy camels and your chimpanzees.
   Noah cried, "Close the door 'cause the rain is pourin',
   And we just can't wait for them unicorn."

5. Then the ark started movin', and it drifted with the tide,
   And the unicorns looked up from the rock and cried.
   And the water come up and sort of floated them away –
   That's why you've never seen a unicorn to this day.
Chorus: You'll see a lot of alligators and a whole mess of geese.
   You'll see humpy bumpy camels and lots of chimpanzees.
   You'll see cats and rats and elephants, but sure as you're born,
   You're never gonna see no unicorn.

You Are My Sunshine

Registration 4
Rhythm: Fox Trot

Words and Music by
Jimmie Davis

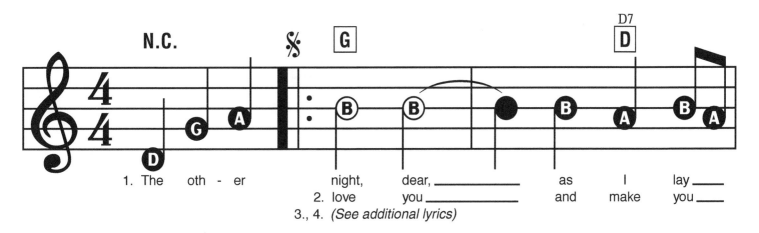

1. The oth - er night, dear, _____ as I lay _____
2. love you _____ and make you _____
3., 4. *(See additional lyrics)*

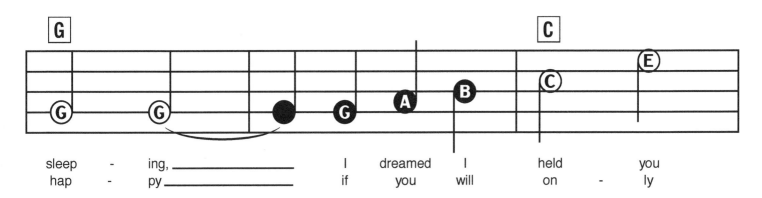

sleep - ing, _____ I dreamed I held you
hap - py _____ if you will on - ly

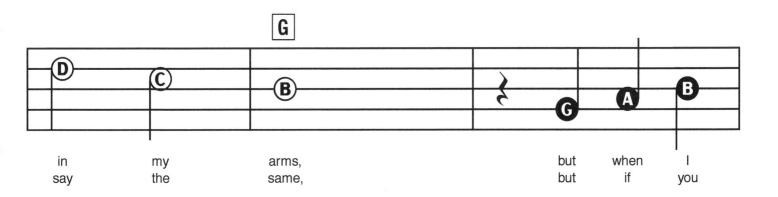

in my arms, but when I
say the same, but if you

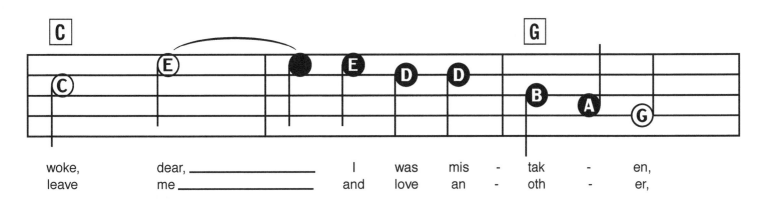

woke, dear, _____ I was mis - tak - en,
leave me _____ and love an - oth - er,

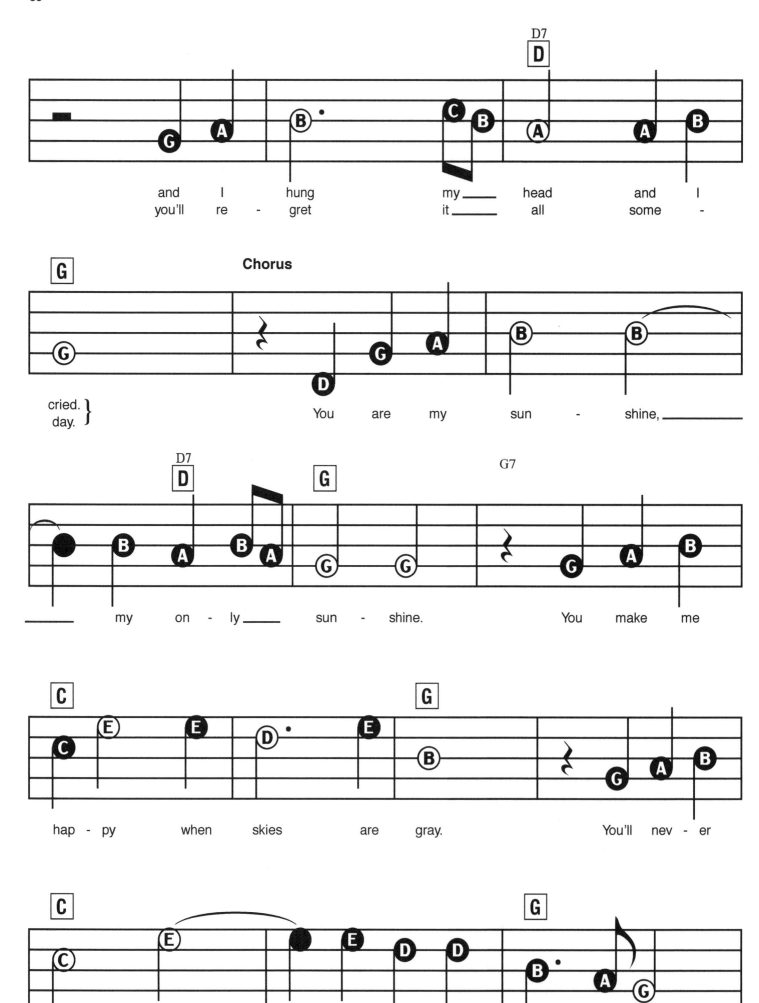

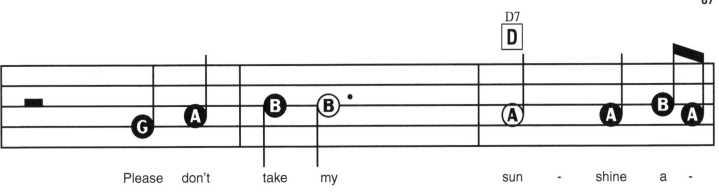

Please don't take my sun - shine a -

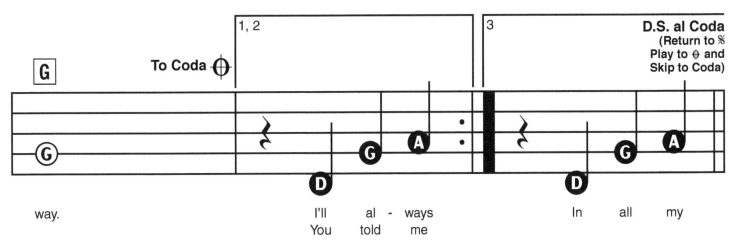

To Coda ⊕   **1, 2**   **3**   **D.S. al Coda**
(Return to ※
Play to ⊕ and
Skip to Coda)

way.   I'll al - ways   In all my
You told me

CODA
⊕

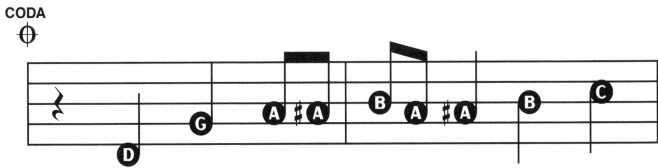

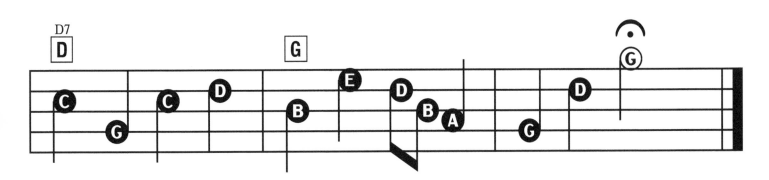

Additional Lyrics

3. You told me once, dear, you really loved me
   And no one could come between,
   But now you've left me to love another.
   You have shattered all of my dreams.
   Chorus

4. In all my dreams, dear, you seem to leave me.
   When I awake my poor heart pains.
   So won't you come back and make me happy?
   I'll forgive, dear; I'll take all the blame.
   Chorus

Registration Guide

- Match the Registration number on the song to the corresponding numbered category below. Select and activate an instrumental sound available on your instrument.

- Choose an automatic rhythm appropriate to the mood and style of the song. (Consult your Owner's Guide for proper operation of automatic rhythm features.)

- Adjust the tempo and volume controls to comfortable settings.

Registration

1	Mellow	Flutes, Clarinet, Oboe, Flugel Horn, Trombone, French Horn, Organ Flutes
2	Ensemble	Brass Section, Sax Section, Wind Ensemble, Full Organ, Theater Organ
3	Strings	Violin, Viola, Cello, Fiddle, String Ensemble, Pizzicato, Organ Strings
4	Guitars	Acoustic/Electric Guitars, Banjo, Mandolin, Dulcimer, Ukulele, Hawaiian Guitar
5	Mallets	Vibraphone, Marimba, Xylophone, Steel Drums, Bells, Celesta, Chimes
6	Liturgical	Pipe Organ, Hand Bells, Vocal Ensemble, Choir, Organ Flutes
7	Bright	Saxophones, Trumpet, Mute Trumpet, Synth Leads, Jazz/Gospel Organs
8	Piano	Piano, Electric Piano, Honky Tonk Piano, Harpsichord, Clavi
9	Novelty	Melodic Percussion, Wah Trumpet, Synth, Whistle, Kazoo, Perc. Organ
10	Bellows	Accordion, French Accordion, Mussette, Harmonica, Pump Organ, Bagpipes